W9-BLR-566

AMERICAN SPORTS POEMS

Read the book.
Write a poem that will
fit into the music of
"Take Me Out To The
Ball Game" on page 31.

AMERICAN SPORTS POEMS

AMERICAN

SPORTS

POEMS

Selected by

R.R. KNUDSON

and

MAY SWENSON

ORCHARD BOOKS

A Division of Franklin Watts, Inc.

NEW YORK

For Alice Quinn, strong swimmer in the sea of poetry.

ORCHARD BOOKS
387 Park Avenue South
New York, New York 10016

ORCHARD BOOKS CANADA
20 Torbay Road
Markham, Ontario 23P 1G6

Orchard Books is a division of Franklin Watts, Inc.
MANUFACTURED IN THE UNITED STATES OF AMERICA
Book design by Tere LoPrete

10 9 8 7 6 5 4 3 2 1

The text of this book is set in 11 pt. Caledonia

Library of Congress Cataloging-in-Publication Data

American sports poems / collected by May Swenson and R.R. Knudson
    p. cm.
    Summary: A collection of poems on sports, ranging from solo
running, hunting, and fighting, to football and baseball from the
spectator's point of view.
    ISBN 0-531-05753-4.   ISBN 0-531-08353-5 (lib. bdg.)
    1. Sports—Juvenile poetry.   2. Children's poetry, American.
[1. Sports—Poetry.   2. American poetry—Collections.]   I. Swenson,
May.   II. Knudson, R. Rozanne, 1932– .
JUV PS595.S78A44 1988
    811'.008'0355—dc19
                                                87-24384
                                                CIP
                                                AC

R00466 19172

Contents

AMERICAN SPORTS POEMS

Catch

Two boys uncoached are tossing a poem together,
Overhand, underhand, backhand, sleight of hand, every hand,
Teasing with attitudes, latitudes, interludes, altitudes,
High, make him fly off the ground for it, low, make him
     stoop,
Make him scoop it up, make him as-almost-as-possible miss it,
Fast, let him sting from it, now, now fool him slowly,
Anything, everything tricky, risky, nonchalant,
Anything under the sun to outwit the prosy,
Over the tree and the long sweet cadence down,
Over his head, make him scramble to pick up the meaning,
And now, like a posy, a pretty one plump in his hands.

Robert Francis

Babe Ruth

He's no Apollo Belvedere
   (That handsome bird of old);
His looks will never raise a cheer
   From females, young or old.
The babies bust out crying when
   They see his fatal block—
But listen, women; listen, men:
   Great
     Gosh
       How he kin
        SOCK!

Damon Runyon

Babe & Lou

when babe hit
number 714 he was
playing for Boston
and washed up

he was a big tipper
a big eater a big
drinker and every
body loved the babe

lou was the iron
man and played
in 2130 consecutive
games and when he coughed
into the microphone
he said he was
the luckiest man alive

he batted clean up
right behind the babe
and together they
represented fear
power and (judging
from the full stands)
absenteeism

this was before the unions
before the depression before
the war and when the smoke

lifted the forties were over and
both men had died slowly
each weighing less
than 100 lbs

Franz Douskey

(5)

Exercise in Preparation for a Pindaric Ode to Carl Hubbell

Long after, Carl,
You will be fabulous: may my song show how!

If but our culture were less disunited,
A poet such as I, "young and promising,"
Might hope to know so great an athlete . . .

O Carl! I saw you once go into Loew's,
After you lost 1–0 to Paul Dean,
And wished to say, Tough luck, Carl Old Boy!
But the words choked in my throat—
              How many times
From Coogan's Bluff as from the walls of Troy
Have I not gazed between the crevices
Of the upper and lower grandstand down below,
In desperate interest and open fear
That a short single would break up the game!

—Spring, immoral Spring, is now upon us,
And in my twenty years of tense devotion
To the great Giant cause, this is the worst
Spring I remember. Bill Jurges, racked
With headaches, on his way to Mayo Clinic,
Terry without a shortstop! But worst of all
The power of the Dodgers who so long
Competed with the comic strips,
                      Alas, Babe Herman,
Ototototoi! Ototototoi! you who once tried
To steal second with the bases loaded!

Delmore Schwartz

Jackie Robinson

ran against walls
without breaking.
in night games
was not foul
but, brave as a hit
over whitestone fences,
entered the conquering dark.

Lucille Clifton

Don Larsen's Perfect Game

Everybody went to bat three times
except their pitcher (twice) and his pinch hitter,
but nobody got anything at all.
Don Larsen in the eighth and ninth looked pale
and afterwards he did not want to talk.
This is a fellow who will have bad dreams.
His catcher Berra jumped for joy and hugged him
like a bear, legs and arms, and all the Yankees
crowded around him thick to make him be
not lonely, and in fact in fact in fact
nothing went wrong. But that was yesterday.

Paul Goodman

Enos Slaughter

my friend's father, I love this story,
all poems are stories

my friend's father was sitting in the stands
in Yankee Stadium with a glass of beer
when "Country" hit one that landed
smackdab in the beer, soaking him
he did not get the ball

innings later, drying, beerdamp, down the front
Country slammed another one
which landed in another of his beers

this second ball
he caught, soaked, but caught
caught and kept

Jim Lavella Havelin

The Kid

One day I watched Ted Williams,
five years after he had left
the Boston Red Sox, five years
after he hit that one last
home run in his last at bat.
He was at his camp in Lakeville
where those who believed in gods
and hoped to be one
went into training for a few weeks
in summer, where you could smell
leather as lovely as roses and hear
the cracks of bats from sunup
to sundown and sometimes later.
There is a picture of Williams
in his World War II pilot's uniform,
the uniform that would keep him
from becoming even greater,
which for Williams would mean
setting even higher standards
for those who followed him.
On this day he looked as he did
in that picture taken some twenty
years earlier: sure of himself,
although some would say cocky.
On this day he was older
and had a paunch, but his hair
was full and black, his eyes clear.
On this day he drove onto the field
in a white Thunderbird
or maybe a Cadillac. I'm not sure.
He leaned on the door of his car,
the car whiter than any baseball,
and watched two college kids
swing for the fences, eternity.

He stepped onto the field
to show them what was wrong
with their swings and they challenged
him to a home run derby.
Five years after he left the Red Sox
he placed his keys on the roof of his car
and said whoever won would drive away.
Maybe Williams needed an edge,
so he used psychology. It doesn't matter.
He drove away.

Kevin Bezner

For Hoyt Wilhelm

the ball dances in
no steam no smoke no
hook across the plate

thrown properly
you see the seams

it doesn't behave
the way it ought to

the sluggers flail away

the catchers lurch
left and right
up and down

if you do hit it
you've got to
make it move
with your own energy
it has so little
of its own

everybody hates it
managers hitters catchers
announcers even complain
it isn't really pitching

the arm lasts
a long time though
and the ball takes
forever to arrive
and the man keeps
throwing it
and no one ever
times it correctly
except by accident
or chance

and if you keep
on doing it
eventually they let you
keep on doing it
even while they hate it

and you keep on and on

the strong arms get tired
the fast balls lose an inch
the curves start hanging
the sliders don't slide

the constants are
the knuckleball
and the wild swings
and you hoyt out there
for a million years
and the e r a
dropping dropping dropping
while the catchers
keep scrambling to stop it

i'm glad you made it

at least one of us guys
with nothing but knucklers
caught their attention

made them say at last
it's the right stuff
even if it does look funny

Joel Oppenheimer

The Last Baseball Samurai

In his final World Series, Pete Rose
wanted to get on base so bad,

he said, that he'd even stick his face
in front of a pitch

if he had to. And he did.
In came Sammy Stewart's hummer.

Out jutted Pete's ugly kisser,
daring the ball to shatter it

if it was capable.
And it was not.

Tom Clark

For the Death of Vince Lombardi

I never played for you. You'd have thrown
Me off the team on my best day—
No guts, maybe   not enough speed,
Yet running in my mind
As Paul Hornung, I made it here
With the others, sprinting down railroad tracks,
Hurdling bushes and backyard Cyclone
Fences, through city after city, to stand, at last, around you,
Exhausted, exalted, pale
As though you'd said "Nice going": pale
As a hospital wall. You are holding us
Millions together: those who played for you,
And those who entered the bodies
Of Bart Starr, Donny Anderson, Ray Nitschke, Jerry Kramer
Through the snowing tube on Sunday afternoon,
Warm, playing painlessly
In the snows of Green Bay Stadium, some of us drunk
On much-advertised beer   some old   some in other
Hospitals—most, middle-aged
And at home. Here you summon us, lying under
The surgical snows. Coach, look up: we are here:
We are held in this room
Like cancer.
The Crab has you, and to him
And to us you whisper
Drive, *Drive*. Jerry Kramer's face floats near—real, pale—
We others dream ourselves
Around you, and far away in the mountains, driving hard
Through the drifts, Marshall of the Vikings, plunging, burning
Twenty-dollar bills to stay alive, says, still
Alive, "I wouldn't be here
If it weren't for the lessons of football." Vince, they've told us;

When the surgeons got themselves
Together and cut loose
Two feet of your large intestine,
The Crab whirled up,   whirled out
Of the lost gut and caught you again
Higher up. Everyone's helpless
But cancer. Around your bed
The knocked-out teeth like hail-pebbles
Rattle down miles of adhesive tape from hands and ankles
Writhe in the room like vines   gallons of sweat
Blaze in buckets
In the corners   the blue and yellow of bruises
Make one vast sunset around you. No one understands you.
Coach, don't you know that some of us were ruined
For life? Everybody can't win. What of almost all
Of us, Vince? We lost.
And our greatest loss was that we could not survive
Football. Paul Hornung has withdrawn
From me, and I am middle-aged and gray like these others.
What holds us here?
It is that you are dying by the code you made us
What we are by? Yes, Coach, it is true: love-hate is stronger
Than either love or hate. Into the weekly, inescapable dance
Of speed, deception, and pain
You led us, and brought us here weeping,
But as men. Or, you who created us as George
Patton created armies, did you discover the worst
In us: aggression, meanness, deception, delight in giving
Pain to others, for money? Did you make of us, indeed,
Figments   overspecialized, brutal ghosts
Who could have been real
Men in a better sense? Have you driven us mad
Over nothing? Does your death set us free?

Too late. We stand here among
Discarded TV commercials:
Among beer cans and razor blades and hair-tonic bottles,
Stinking with male deodorants: we stand here
Among teeth and filthy miles
Of unwound tapes, novocaine needles, contracts, champagne
Mixed with shower water,
Unraveling elastic, bloody face guards,
And the Crab, in his new, high position
Works soundlessly. In dying
You give us no choice, Coach,
Either. We've got to believe there's such a thing
As winning. The Sunday spirit-screen
Comes on   the bruise-colors brighten   deepen
On the wall   the last tooth spits itself free
Of a linebacker's aging head   knee cartilage cracks,
A boy wraps his face in a red jersey and crams it into
A rusty locker to sob, and we're with you
We're with you all the way
You're going forever, Vince.

James Dickey

Unitas

Dignified and thin
he gathered in the snap
and glided back a good twelve yards
and stopped and set and hit
a place in time and space
where Raymond Berry hung
and grabbed it out of air
and touched his toetops in
as he went out.

Not our father or friend,
he was a wizard who led us,
brilliant in the distance
he demanded and kept from us,
bringing sudden death to Giants
or dazzling the Bears.

We loved his grace,
and trusted his eyes,
his arm,
his spindly legs,
backpedaling him away
from red dogs and blitzes,
and all of us,
to pass from the pocket.

Edward Gold

Billy Ray Smith

Who's been squashing Billy Ray Smith?
Who has he been tangling with?
His fellow Colts go charging by
To block that Falcon field goal try,
But somewhere, somehow, Billy Ray
Got turned around the other way.
Mostly this towering human redwood
Crumbles the opposite line like deadwood,
So he can't be turning the other cheek—
Not with his temperament and physique.

Ogden Nash

Say Goodbye to Big Daddy

Big Daddy Lipscomb, who used to help them up
After he'd pulled them down, so that "the children
Won't think Big Daddy's mean"; Big Daddy Lipscomb,
Who stood unmoved among the blockers, like the Rock
Of Gibraltar in a life insurance ad,
Until the ball carrier came, and Daddy got him;
Big Daddy Lipscomb, being carried down an aisle
Of women by Night Train Lane, John Henry Johnson,
And Lenny Moore; Big Daddy, his three ex-wives,
His fiancée, and the grandfather who raised him
Going to his grave in five big Cadillacs;
Big Daddy, who found football easy enough, life hard enough
To—after his last night cruising Baltimore
In his yellow Cadillac—to die of heroin;
Big Daddy, who was scared, he said: "I've been scared
Most of my life. You wouldn't think so to look at me.
It gets so bad I cry myself to sleep—" his size
Embarrassed him, so that he was helped by smaller men
And hurt by smaller men; Big Daddy Lipscomb
Has helped to his feet the last ball carrier, Death.

The big black man in the television set
Whom the viewers stared at—sometimes, almost were—
Is a blur now; when we get up to adjust the set,
It's not the set, but a NETWORK DIFFICULTY.
The world won't be the same without Big Daddy.
Or else it will be.

Randall Jarrell

High Stick

Bobby Orr's marble
head, hard and blue

as the ice he skates

his face,
the penalty of stitches.

Billy Collins

Wilt Chamberlain

Wilt was so built
he could give it a tilt
over the rim
hardly higher than him.

Does Wilty feel guilty
he's not that trim
in girth and limb
as when he was slim?

Old age is grim.

Now, much like Joe
DiMaggio
Wilty is seen
on the TV screen
with an easy laugh
folding in half.

He's doing a plug
for the Volkswagen Bug
to prove it's wide
enough, tall, and more so,
for Wilt's famous torso
to fit inside.

R. R. Knudson

Patrick Ewing
Takes a Foul Shot

Ewing sweating,
molding the ball
with spidery hands,
packing it, packing it,
into a snowball's
chance of a goal,
rolling his shoulders
through a silent earthquake,
rocking from one foot
to the other, sweating,
bouncing it, oh, sweet
honey, molding it,
packing it tight,
he fires:

floats it up on one palm
as if surfacing
from the clear green Caribbean
with a shell
whose roar wraps around him,
whose surf breaks
deep into his arena
where light and time
and pupils jump
because he jumps

Diane Ackerman

Sonja Henie Sonnet

In high school we danced the lindy white-style
like Sonja Henie on her skates
curvetting her way around the rinky-dink
back-first, front-first, leaving a trail of scars.

Splitting in air or dissolving in a spin
she came out holding her muff to cheeks
dimpled and rosy under Bo-Peep bonnet
as snowflakes starred her blond and marcelled head,

and curtsying, her little behind
peek-a-booed under fluffy skirt
when she braked to a stop before the cameras
in a cloud of powdery ice.

Below, blunt feet in leather with blades of steel
dug in their points and held.

Edward Field

Blues for Benny Kid Paret

For years I've watched the corners for signs.
A hook, a jab, a feint, the peekaboo prayer of forearms,
anything for the opening, the rematch I go on dreaming.
What moves can say your life is saved?

    As I backpedaled in a field the wasp's nest waited,
    playing another game: a child is peeping out of
    my eyes now, confused by the madness of stinging,
    wave after wave rising as I tell my fists punish me,
    counter the pain. I take my own beating and God help

    me it hurts. Everything hurts, every punch
    jolts, rips my ears, my cheeks, my temples. Who hurts
    a man faster than himself? There was a wall to bounce
    on, better than ropes. I was eleven years old.

Eleven years age I saw the fog
turn away and rise from the welts you were
to run away with its cousin the moon. They smacked

your chest and crossed your arms because you fell down
while the aisles filled with gorgeous women, high heels
pounding like Emile, the Champion, who planted his
good two feet and stuck, stuck, stuck, stuck
until your brain tied up your tongue and sighed.

    Somebody please, please I cried
    make them go away, but the ball in my hand had turned
    feverish with its crackling light. I could not let go
    as I broke against the wall. I was eleven years old.

Benny Paret, this night in a car ferrying
my load of darkness like a ring no one escapes,
I am bobbing and weaving in fog split only by a radio
whose harsh gargle is eleven years old, a voice in the air

telling the night you are down, counting time,
and I hear other voices from corners with bad moves say
Get up, you son of a bitch, get up! But you will not
get up again in my life where the only sign you give me

is a moon I remember sailing down on your heart
and blood growing wings to fly up in your eyes.
And there, there the punches no one feels grow weak,
as the wall looms, break through the best prayer you had
to dump you dizzied and dreaming in the green grass.

Dave Smith

Babe Didrikson

From the high jump of Olympic fame,
The hurdles and the rest,
The javelin that flashed its flame
On by the record test—
The Texas Babe now shifts the scene
Where slashing drives are far
Where spoon shots find the distant green
To break the back of par.

Grantland Rice

Never Be As Fast As I Have Been

the jockey Tony DeSpirito dead at thirty-nine

When Tony was found dead in his
walk-up apartment, there were few who knew him.
A nobody. A loser. Illusory and obscure
as a third-rate poet. But in reality

the boy was so renowned the track announcer
called the rider instead of the horse—
and here comes Tony DeSpirito
flying like the wind on the outside

Spilled nine times, he had the last
rites twice and lost a kidney & spleen.
To come back was hard. To pass unnoticed
to the fanciful world of wages was tempting,

having won at the age of sixteen
four hundred races in a single year.
He made the cover of *Time* magazine.
A genius. The Kid! One of the immortals

like Delmore Schwartz. He lived in the end
on french fries and scotch, and crossed
with fabulous speed to the other shore
from an unreal place in Riverside, R.I.

Robert Hahn

Prefontaine

He wore old Oregon on his chest,
a new mustache on his 24-year-old lip
and a scowl on his brow
that could jump out his mouth
quicker than that famous final kick.
We all agreed
he could run and run and run
after women and whiskey and ribbons,
a chip off the old lumberjack block.
We in the stands gave our clapped-red hands
to him and his victory laps.
We watched and prayed for his rugged runty form
under suns, gym ceilings and television rooms.
He stood us wild after each mile
witnessing his sudden bursts of speed.
We curse a coffin car we never saw.

Charles Ghigna

Joan Benoit

1984 U.S. Olympic Marathon Gold Medalist

During the third mile
not the eighteenth as expected
she surged ahead
leaving behind the press
of bodies, the breath
hot on her back
and set a pace
the experts claimed
she couldn't possibly keep
to the end.

Sure, determined,
moving to an inner rhythm
measuring herself against herself
alone in a field of fifty
she gained the twenty-six miles
of concrete, asphalt and humid weather
and burst into the roar of the crowd
to run the lap around the stadium
at the same pace
once to finish the race
and then again in victory

and she was still fresh
and not even out of breath
and standing.

Rina Ferrarelli

Take Me Out to the Ball Game

Take me out to the ball game,
Take me out with the crowd,
Buy me some peanuts and Cracker-jack,
I don't care if I never get back.
Let me root, root, root for the home team,
If they don't win it's a shame,
For it's one, two, three strikes you're out,
At the old ball game

Jack Norworth

Analysis of Baseball

It's about
the ball,
the bat,
and the mitt.
Ball hits
bat, or it
hits mitt.
Bat doesn't
hit ball, bat
meets it.
Ball bounces
off bat, flies
air, or thuds
ground (dud)
or it
fits mitt.

Bat waits
for ball
to mate.
Ball hates
to take bat's
bait. Ball
flirts, bat's
late, don't
keep the date.
Ball goes in
(thwack) to mitt,
and goes out
(thwack) back
to mitt.

Ball fits
mitt, but
not all
the time.
Sometimes
ball gets hit
(pow) when bat
meets it,
and sails
to a place
where mitt
has to quit
in disgrace.
That's about
the bases
loaded,
about 40,000
fans exploded.

It's about
the ball,
the bat,
the mitt,
the bases
and the fans.
It's done
on a diamond,
and for fun.
It's about
home, and it's
about run.

May Swenson

Hits and Runs

I remember the Chillicothe ball players grappling the Rock
        Island ball players in a sixteen-inning game ended by
        darkness.

And the shoulders of the Chillicothe players were a red smoke
        against the sundown and the shoulders of the Rock
        Island players were a yellow smoke against the sun-
        down.

And the umpire's voice was hoarse calling balls and strikes
        and outs, and the umpire's throat fought in the
        dust for a song.

Carl Sandburg

The Origin of Baseball

Someone had been walking in and out
Of the world without coming
To much decision about anything.
The sun seemed too hot most of the time.
There weren't enough birds around
And the hills had a silly look
When he got on top of one.
The girls in heaven, however, thought
Nothing of asking to see his watch
Like you would want someone to tell
A joke—"Time," they'd say, "what's
That mean—time?" laughing with the edges
Of their white mouths, like a flutter of paper
In a madhouse. And he'd stumble over
General Sherman or Elizabeth B.
Browning, muttering, "Can't you keep
Your big wings out of the aisle?" But down
Again, there'd be millions of people without
Enough to eat and men with guns just
Standing there shooting each other.

So he wanted to throw something
And he picked up a baseball.

Kenneth Patchen

Instruction

The coach has taught her how to swing,
run bases, slide, how to throw
to second, flip off her mask for fouls.

Now, on her own, she studies
how to knock the dirt out of her cleats,
hitch up her pants, miss her shoulder
with a stream of spit, bump
her fist into her catcher's mitt,
and stare incredulously at the ump.

Conrad Hilberry

Let's Go, Mets

Opening of the 1984 Season

Mookie and Hubie and Strawberry,
These are the guys in the lineup for me.
Hernandez can hit, play first base with style,
Foster comes through every once in a while.
But for hustle and muscle and artistry,
Give me Mookie and Hubie and Strawberry.
These are my hopefuls, these are my three:
Mookie and Hubie and Strawberry.

Lillian Morrison

Baseball Canto

Watching baseball
sitting in the sun
eating popcorn
reading Ezra Pound

and wishing Juan Marichal
would hit a hole right through
the Anglo-Saxon tradition
in the First Canto
and demolish the barbarian invaders

When the San Francisco Giants take the field
and everybody stands up to the National Anthem
with some Irish tenor's voice
piped over the loudspeakers
with all the players struck dead in their places
and the white umpires like Irish cops
in their black suits and little black caps
pressed over their hearts
standing straight and still
like at some funeral of a blarney bartender
and all facing East
as if expecting some Great White Hope
or the Founding Fathers
to appear on the horizon
like 1066 or 1776 or all that

But Willie Mays appears instead
in the bottom of the first
and a roar goes up
         as he clouts the first one into the sun
            and takes off
               like a footrunner from Thebes
      The ball is lost in the sun
            and maidens wail after him

                              but he keeps running
                                        through the Anglo-Saxon epic

And Tito Fuentes comes up
            looking like a bullfighter
            in his tight pants and small pointed shoes

And the rightfield bleachers go mad
                with chicanos & blacks & Brooklyn beerdrinkers
                        "Sweet Tito! Sock it to heem, Sweet Tito!"
And Sweet Tito puts his foot in the bucket
                and smacks one that don't come back at all
                and flees around the bases
        like he's escaping from the United Fruit Company
            as the gringo dollar beats out the Pound
                and Sweet Tito beats it out
                like he's beating out usury
                not to mention fascism and anti-semitism

And Juan Marichal comes up
    and the chicano bleachers go loco again
        as Juan belts the first fast ball
                out of sight
                    and rounds first and keeps going
            and rounds second and rounds third
                            and keeps going
                            and hits pay-dirt
            to the roars of the grungy populace
As some nut presses the backstage panic button
for the tape-recorded National Anthem again
to save the situation

but it don't stop nobody this time
in their revolution round the loaded white bases
in this last of the great Anglo-Saxon epics
in the *Territorio Libre* of baseball

        Lawrence Ferlinghetti

I've Never Written a Baseball Poem

For Reuben Jackson, who has

I didn't even make
the seventh grade
girls' third team

substitute.
Still can't
throw straight.

Last Easter, scrub game
with the kids,
I hit

a foul right through
Captain Kelly's French doors,
had to pay.

Still, these sultry
country nights
I watch

the dark ballet
of players sliding
into base,

and shout "Safe!
He's safe! He's home!"
and so am I.

Elisavietta Ritchie

Casey's Daughter at the Bat

The outlook wasn't brilliant for the Mudvillettes, it seems;
The score stood four to two against that best of softball teams;
And when Brenda ("Lefty") Cooney and "Babs" Barrows both
    flied out,
A sickly silence filled the air, and the fans began to pout.

A straggling few got up to go—'twas the ninth and two were
    down—
While the rest had little hope at all that the 'Ettes would Go
    To Town;
Still, they thought if only Casey's gal—Patricia—Patsy—Pat—
Could get a lick, they still might win with Casey at the bat.

But Myrna Flynn and Hedy Blake had to hit before Miss C.;
And the former was a sissy, and the latter just a she;
So again upon a Mudville throng grim melancholy sat,
For there seemed no chance whatever that Patricia'd get to
    bat.

But Myrna smacked a single, to the wonderment of all,
And Hedy—known as Flatfoot—fairly flattened out the ball;
And when the dust had lifted, there on third and second base
Perched a pair of Mudville cuties, each a-powdering her face.

Then from the howling mamas in the stand in back of first
Went up a weird, unearthly scream, like a Tarzan crazed with
    thirst,
Like a million screeching monkey-fans, like a yowling giant
    cat:
For Casey, Patsy Casey, was advancing to the bat!

There was ease in Patsy's manner as she stepped up to the
    plate;
There were curves in Patsy's figure, and a bounce in Patsy's
    gait;

And when responding to the screams she lightly doffed her
    hat,
No Casey fan could doubt 'twas Mighty's daughter at the bat.

Ten thousand eyes were on her shorts, an orchidaceous hue;
Five thousand tongues commented on her blouse of beige-
    and-blue;
And while the ladies chattered "What a shape!" and "What a
    fit!"
Miss Casey gave her shorts a tug and smoothed her blouse a
    bit.

And now the underhanded pitch came hurtling through the
    air,
But Patsy, like her famous dad, just stood a-smiling there;
And when "Strike one!" the umpire yelled as past that softball
    sped,
"That ain't my style!" is what they say Patricia Casey said.

Again, as in the years a-gone, the crowd set up a roar;
Again, they shouted as they had so many years before,
"Kill him! kill the umpire!"; and as once did Patsy's Pop,
Miss Casey raised a staying hand, and mildly said, "Oh, stop!"

And smiling like a lady in a teethy toothpaste ad,
Patricia showed that howling mob she wasn't even mad;
She signaled to the pitcher, who again the ball let fly;
And again like Papa Casey's, Patsy's second strike went by.

Anew, the maddened thousands blamed the strike upon the
    ump;
A racketeer, they labeled him, a floogie, and a frump;
But once again the mob was stilled by Patsy's charming smile,
As certain every fan became she'd hit the next a mile.

And now they see her daub a bit of powder on her nose;
They watch her put fresh lipstick on—a shade called Fleur de
    Rose;

And now the pitcher holds the ball, and now she lets it go;
And now the air is shattered by *another* Casey's blow.

Oh! somewhere in this favored land the moon is shining
    bright;
And somewhere there are softball honeys winning games
    tonight.
And somewhere there are softball fans who scream and yell
    and shout;
But there's still no joy in Mudville—Casey's *daughter* has
    struck out.

Al Graham

Clothespins

I once hit clothespins
for the Chicago Cubs.
I'd go out after supper
when the wash was in
and collect clothespins
from under four stories
of clothesline.
A swing-and-a-miss
was a strike-out;
the garage roof, Willie Mays,
pounding his mitt
under a pop fly.
Bushes, a double,
off the fence, triple,
and over, home run.
The bleachers roared.
I was all they ever needed
for the flag.
New records every game—
once, 10 homers in a row!
But sometimes I'd tag them
so hard they'd explode,
legs flying apart in midair,
pieces spinning crazily
in all directions.
Foul Ball! What else
could I call it?
The bat was real.

Stuart Dybek

(43)

In My Meanest Daydream

I am throwing hard again
clipping corners, shaving
letters, dusting off
the heavy sticker crowding clean-up
clean down to his smelly socks—
& when my right spike hits
the ground he's had his
look already & gets
hollow in the belly—
in my meanest daydream I let fly
a sweet stream of spit, my catcher
pops his mitt
& grins
& calls me baby.

Gary Gildner

Sacrifice Bunt

You hold the bat at eye-level,
knees bent, get down to meet the ball,
preparing to give yourself up
for the common good.
Your bat is an extension of the body,
the idea being to catch the ball
with all you have.
Somebody is depending on you
to move him along, a vulnerable friend,
the kind of guy who wonders in sweat
WHAT AM I DOING HERE.
A limbo of wind comes off the mound,
nothing but a tiny marble
small enough for a navel.
Squared, you have given yourself away,
each rotation of the ball saying
NO PLACE TO HIDE
NO PLACE
NO
O
You can't think about it,
about popping it up.
Suddenly it's on the ground, he's safe,
you're out, he's in scoring position,
you're on the bench, you've left it up
to the next guy, the reader.

Lucky Jacobs

Softball Dreams

I did not know why I liked it, all the waiting,
then the ball falling from the sky
smacking my glove, forcing from it
a scent like a shoe's inside,
the glove's new lacing creaking
like ship rigging.

I studied the sky above
the bill of my red cap,
the jets detailed as toys
that crossed silently
but seemed near collision,
the shrieking birds that were a river
of black beating shapes. One night
the sky and the dirt were the same color.
I moved with the ease of a swimmer
through the cool ruddy element,
the ball always a surprise
rushing into my face.

All women, we began playing in the evening
in those long hours after dinner.
Considering each other
only according to skill, we played
until the sun, orange and solid,
was eclipsed by trees. At the edge
of the diamond our children spraddled,
through fists trickling sand
filling bottles.

On the hot nights I would wake
uncertain in my own bed
as if standing on a midnight riverbank,
water sensed
by its sheen through trees.

The schoolyard was enclosed
by maroon brick houses, their small porches
overflowing with red and purple petunias.
Each pavement crack was tufted
with spider-rampant grass.
A dense season, the air thick
with moisture and kicked-up dust,
overripe figs in the alleys dangling
under the coarse, splayed leaves.

When we could no longer close our dry mouths
we'd go to a bar where a mirrored ball
revolved in green light, its phosphorescence
shattering on our faces, and beneath
the feet of the dancers
who pulled near each other,
without intensity, underwater.

Karen Kevorkian

Listening to Baseball in the Car

for James Tate

This morning I argued with a friend
about angels. I didn't believe
in his belief in them—I can't
believe they're not a metaphor.
Our argument, affectionate,
lacking in animus, went nowhere.
We promised to talk again soon.
Now, when I'm driving away
from Boston and the Red Sox
are losing, I hear the announcer
say, "No angels in the sky today"—
baseball-ese for *a cloudless afternoon,*
no shadows to help a man
who waits in the outfield
staring into the August sun.
Although I know the announcer's
not a rabbi or sage (no,
he's a sort of sage, disconsolate
philosopher of batting slumps
and injuries), still I scan
the pale blue sky through my
polarized windshield, fervently
hopeful for my fading team
and I feel something a little
foolish, a prayerful throbbing
in my throat and remember
being told years ago that men
are only little lower than
the angels. Floating ahead of me
at the Vermont border, I see

a few wispy horsemane clouds
which I quietly pray will drift
down to Fenway Park where
a demonic opponent has just
slammed another Red Sox pitch,
and the center fielder—call him Jim—
runs back, back, back,
looking heavenward,
and is shielded and doesn't lose
the white ball in the glare.

Gail Mazur

World Champions

A cardinal is perched upon a bat
Upon a pennant on a pole upon a field: that
Means you pay to see
The redbirds warming up: this is baseball.

All but a few of us waited weeks
For the occasion: so tonight
There is nothing disconcerting in the sight
Of these birdmen whose redbills might be beaks.

The game begins: and not for want of nerve
The Giant is defeated by a slingshot throw
Which cuts across the diamond like a flaw,
Like light across the Tablets of the Law,
Or thunder when the high blue heavens yield:

A cardinal is perched upon a bat;
A cardinal is perched upon a field.

William Jay Smith

Right Where He Left Off

Big Willie's back from the war
and still he loves a ball game.
You should see him play:
cap pulled low on his forehead,
glove oiled, the cleats he wore
his three seasons All-State shined.
And Willie's hustling never stops.
Even after the game he's got me running
back to the van. And believe me,
it's hell wheeling that damn chair.

Craig Weeden

Couplet

Old Timers' Day, Fenway Park, 1 May 1982

When the tall puffy
figure wearing number
nine starts
late for the fly ball,
laboring forward
like a lame truckhorse
startled by a gartersnake,
—this old fellow
whose body we remember
as sleek and nervous
as a filly's—

and barely catches it
in his glove's
tip, we rise
and applaud weeping:
On a green field
we observe the ruin
of even the bravest
body, as Odysseus
wept to glimpse
among shades the shadow
of Achilles.

Donald Hall

The Song of Snohomish

Catfish, Mudcat, Ducky, Coot.
The Babe, The Barber, The Blade, The Brat.
Windy, Dummy, Gabby, Hoot.
Big Train, Big Six, Big Ed, Fat.

Greasy, Sandy, Muddy, Rocky.
Bunions, Twinkletoes, Footsie. The Hat.
Fuzzy, Dizzy, Buddy, Cocky.
The Bull, The Stork, The Weasel, The Cat.

    Schoolboy, Preacher,
    Rajah, Duke
    General, Major,
    Spaceman, Spook.

Shoeless Joe, Cobra Joe, Bullet Joe.
Bing.
Old Hoss, Mule, Country, Rube.
Smokey Joe, Fireman Joe, Jersey Joe.
Ping.
Bulldog, Squirrel, Puddin' Head, Boob.

The Georgia Peach, The Fordham Flash.
The Flying Dutchman. Cot.
The People's Cherce, The Blazer. Crash.
The Staten Island Scot.

    Skeeter, Scooter,
    Pepper, Duster,
    Ebba, Bama, Boomer, Buster.

Specs.
The Grey Eagle, The Toy Cannon.
Tex.
The Earl of Snohomish, The Duke of Tralee.
Art the Great; Gorgeous George.
Ox. Double X.
The Nashville Narcissus. The Phantom. The Flea.

(53)

The Little Professor, The Iron Horse. Cap.
Iron Man, Iron Mike, Iron Hands. Hutch.
Jap, The Mad Russian, Irish, Swede. Nap.
Germany, Frenchy, Big Serb, Dutch,
    Turk
        Tuck. Tug. Twig.
     Spider, Birdie, Rabbit, Pig.

Three-Finger, No-Neck, The Knuck, The Lip.
Casey, Dazzy, Hippity. Zim.
Flit, Bad Henry. Fat Freddie, Flip.
Jolly Cholly. Sunny Jim.

    Shag, Schnozz,
    King Kong, Klu.
    Boog, Buzz,
    Boots, Bump, Boo.

Baby Doll, Angel Sleeves, Pep, Sliding Billy,
Buttercup, Bollicky, Boileryard, Juice,
Colby Jack, Dauntless Dave, Cheese, Gentle Willie,
Trolley Line, Wagon Tongue, Rough, What's the Use.

    Ee-yah,
    Poosh 'Em Up,
    Skoonj, Slats, Ski.
    Ding Dong,
    Ding-a-Ling,
    Dim Dom, Dee.

Bubbles, Dimples, Cuddles, Pinky.
Poison Ivy, Vulture, Stinky.
    Jigger, Jabbo
    Jolting Joe
    Blue Moon
    Boom Boom
    Bubba
    Bo.

        William S. Wallace
(For answers, see page 205)

Heart

from Damn Yankees

You've gotta have heart
All you really need is heart
When the odds are sayin' you'll never win,
That's when the grin should start.
You've gotta have hope
Mustn't sit around and mope
Nothin's half as bad as it may appear
Wait'll next year and hope.
When you luck is battin' zero
Get your chin up off the floor;
Mister you can be a hero
You can open any door, there's nothin' to it, but to do it.
You've gotta have heart
Miles 'n miles 'n miles of heart
Oh, it's fine to be a genius of course
But keep that old horse
Before the cart
First you've gotta have heart.

Richard Adler and Jerry Ross

(55)

The Notre Dame Victory March

Cheer, cheer for old Notre Dame.
Wake up the echoes cheering her name,
Send a volley cheer on high,
Shake down the thunder from the sky.
What though the odds be great or small?
Old Notre Dame will win over all,
While her loyal sons are marching
Onward to victory.

John Shea

Football

Now they're ready, now they're waiting,
Now he's going to place the ball.
There, you hear the referee's whistle,
As of old the baton's fall.
See him crouching. Yes, he's got it;
Now he's off around the end.
Will the interference save him?
Will the charging line now bend?
Good, he's free; no, see that halfback
Gaining up behind him slow.
Crash! they're down; he threw him nicely,—
Classy tackle, hard and low.
Watch that line, now crouching waiting,
In their jerseys white and black;
Now they're off and charging, making
Passage for the plunging back.
Buck your fiercest, run your fastest,
Let the straight arm do the rest.
Oh, they got him; never mind, though,
He could only do his best.
What is this? A new formation.
Look! their end acts like an ass.
See, he's beckoning for assistance,
Maybe it's a forward pass.
Yes, the ball is shot to fullback,
He, as calmly as you please,
Gets it, throws it to the end; he
Pulls the pigskin down with ease.
Now they've got him. No, they haven't.
See him straight-arm all those fools.
Look, he's clear. Oh, gee! don't stumble.
Faster, faster, for the school.
There's the goal, now right before you,
Ten yards, five yards, bless your name!
Oh! you Newman, 1911,
You know how to play the game.

F. Scott Fitzgerald

Dedicated to F. W.

Lives of football men remind us,
   We can dive and kick and slug,
And departing leave behind us,
   Hoof prints on another's mug.

Ernest Hemingway

The Sleeper

When I was the sissy of the block who nobody wanted on
    their team
Sonny Hugg persisted in believing that my small size was an
    asset
Not the liability and curse I felt it was
And he saw a use for my swift feet with which I ran away
    from fights.

He kept putting me into complicated football plays
Which would have been spectacular if they worked:
For instance, me getting clear in front and him shooting the
    ball over—
Or the sensation of the block, the Sleeper Play
In which I would lie down on the sidelines near the goal
As though resting and out of action, until the scrimmage
    began
And I would step onto the field, receive the long throw
And to the astonishment of all the tough guys in the world
Step over the goal line for a touchdown

That was the theory anyway. In practice
I had the fatal flaw of not being able to catch
And usually had my fingers bend back and the breath
    knocked out of me
So the plays always failed, but Sonny kept on trying
Until he grew up out of my world into the glamorous
Varsity crowd, the popular kids of Lynbrook High.

But I will always have this to thank him for:
That when I look back on childhood
(That four psychiatrists haven't been able to help me bear the
    thought of)
There is not much to be glad for
Besides his foolish and delicious faith
That, with all my oddities, there was a place in the world for
    me
If only he could find the special role.

Edward Field

Watching Football on TV

I

It used to be only Sunday afternoons,
But people have got more devoted now
And maybe three four times a week retire
To their gloomy living room to sit before
The polished box alive with silver light
And moving shadows, that incessantly
Gives voice, even when pausing for messages.
The colored shadows made of moving light,
The voice that ritually recites the sense
Of what they do, enter a myriad minds.
Down on the field, massed bands perform the anthem
Sung by a soprano invisible elsewhere;
Sometimes a somewhat neutral public prayer—
For in the locker rooms already both
Sides have prayed God to give them victory.

I I

Totemic scarabs, exoskeletal,
Nipped in at the thorax, bulky above and below,
With turreted hard heads and jutting masks
And emblems of the lightning or the beast;
About the size of beetles in our sight,
Save for the closeup and the distant view,
Yet these are men, our representatives
More formidable than ourselves in speed and strength
And preparation, and more injured too;
Bandage and cast exhibit breakages
Incurred in wars before us played before;
Hard plaster makes a weapon of an arm,
A calf becomes a club. Now solemnly
They take up their positions in the light
And soon their agon will begin again.

III

To all this there are rules. The players must
Remember that in the good society
Grabbing at anybody's mask will be
A personal foul and incur a penalty.
So too will pushing, tripping, interfering
In any manner with someone else's pass.
Fighting is looked on with particular
Severity; though little harm can come
To people so plated at shoulder, head and thigh,
The most conspicuous offenders are
Ejected from the game and even fined.
That's one side of the coin, the other one
Will bear the picture of a charging bull
Or some such image imprecating fear,
And for its legend have the one word: *Kill.*

IV

Priam on one side sending forth eleven
Of many sons, and Agamemnon on
The other doing much the same; is it
The Game of Troy again? the noble youth
Fiery with emulation, maneuvering
Toward power and preeminence? Well no,
It's not. Money is the name of the game
From the board room to the beers and souvenirs.
The players are mean and always want more money.
The owners are mean and always have more money
And mean to keep it while the players go
Out there to make them more; they call themselves
Sportsmen, they own, are and carry a club.
Remember this when watching the quarterback's
Suppliant hands under the center's butt.

V

We watch all afternoon, we are enthralled
To what? some drama of the body and
The intellectual soul? of strategy
In its rare triumphs and frequent pratfalls?
The lucid playbook in the memory
Wound up in a spaghetti of arms and legs
Waving above a clump of trunks and rumps
That slowly sorts itself out into men?
That happens many times. But now and then
The runner breaks into the clear and goes,
The calm parabola of a pass completes
Itself like destiny, giving delight
Not only at skill but also at the sight
Of men who imitate necessity
By more than meeting its immense demands.

V I

Passing and catching overcome the world,
The hard condition of the world, they do
Human intention honor in the world.
A football wants to wobble, that's its shape
And nature, and to make it spiral true
's a triumph in itself, to make it hit
The patterning receiver on the hands
The instant he looks back, well, that's to be
For the time being in a state of grace,
And move the viewers in their living rooms
To lost nostalgic visions of themselves
As in an earlier, other world where grim
Fate in the form of gravity may be
Not merely overcome, but overcome
Casually and with style, and that is grace.

VII

Each year brings rookies and makes veterans,
They have their dead by now, their wounded as well,
They have Immortals in a Hall of Fame,
They have the stories of the tribe, the plays
And instant replays many times replayed.
But even fame will tire of its fame,
And immortality itself will fall asleep.
It's taken many years, but yet in time,
To old men crouched before the ikon's changes,
Changes become reminders, all the games
Are blended in one vast remembered game
Of similar images simultaneous
And superposed; nothing surprises us
Nor can delight, though we see the tight end
Stagger into the end zone again again.

Howard Nemerov

Watching the Jets Lose to Buffalo at Shea

The feel of that leather baby
solid against your sternum,
you hug its skull and bottom
between huge huddled shoulders.
It's wrapped in your arms and wedged
under the hard muzzle
of your stuck-out faceguard.

Your thighs pumping, you run
to deliver the baby
to a cradle of grass at the goalposts.
But it's bumped from your arms,
and you're mounted
as if your back were leather.
Your legs cut away, you fold,

you tumble like a treetrunk.
Your brain's for the ground to split
like a leather egg, but it doesn't.
Your helmet takes the concussion.
Sent aloft by a leather toe,
a rugged leather baby
dropped from the sky and slammed

into the sling of your arms.
Oh, the feel of that leather bundle.
Oh, what a blooper and fumbler
you are, that you couldn't nest it,
that you lost and couldn't nurse it,
long enough to lay it
in a cradle of grass at the goalposts.

May Swenson

Marvin Pickett

When I wear my football jersey to class
All the foxes give me the eye.
I am number one, the best there is.
Ain't nobody like me in the history of the school.
I am the greatest pass receiver in the world.
Last Saturday I faked two defenders out of their sneakers
And caught the touchdown that won the game.
School's for fillin' in the week, man.
On the football field I'm king.
Got it all figured out: two years J.C. ball,
Then college,
Then the draft,
Then the pros.
Hey, man, don't you believe me?
Ain't you listenin'?
I'm the best there is.

Mel Glenn

You've Got to Learn
the White Man's Game

for Taylor

the 5th black law student
at the university of missouri
squats, away from the grandstands,
at the top of a hill
whistling a jazz tune.
the football game bored him to murder,
the lions & christians, the christians, esp.
the gladiators, the whole show
with red necks in little red caps
shouting, "go, go, Nebraska, big red."
he could tell 'em 'bout red.
he dreamed in that color.

take it up the sideline, cut back,
down the middle, shove it
down their throats
stand at home plate smiling,
connect with a right & dance
above their slumped bodies.
he dreamed in red, blood red.
"But Not For Me" he whistled consciously
as he sat on his haunches
at the top of the hill
& let the cold whip
the back of his neck.
he would play the game,
be a cool honcho,
play the game.

he would squat
at the top of the hill
& maybe convince himself
it's all sport.

Mbembe Milton Smith

(67)

To the Field Goal Kicker in a Slump

It must be something
like writer's block,
when nothing will go
between the margins,
when language won't soar
high enough,
when you wake
in the morning and know
you've chosen
the wrong game.

Linda Pastan

Insanity

Hit!

Smash

Guts,

Butts,

Crush

Heads.

Break

Legs,

Arms,

Backs.

Men

In stacks,

All

After a ball.

Gaston Dubois

In the Pocket

Going backward
All of me and some
Of my friends are forming a shell   my arm is looking
Everywhere and some are breaking
In   breaking down
And out   breaking
Across, and one is going deep   deeper
Than my arm.   Where is Number One hooking
Into the violent green alive
With linebackers?   I cannot find him he cannot beat
His man   I fall back more
Into the pocket   it is raging and breaking
Number Two has disappeared into the chalk
Of the sideline   Number Three is cutting with half
A step of grace   my friends are crumbling
Around me the wrong color
Is looming   hands are coming
Up and over between
My arm and Number Three: throw it hit him in
the middle
Of his enemies   hit move scramble
Before death and the ground
Come up   LEAP STAND KILL DIE STRIKE
Now.

James Dickey

Meeting My Best Friend
from the Eighth Grade

He says when he comes in a bar
after beating Wyoming, say,
there's something like fur in the air
and people don't see him, they see a bear.

My best friend from the eighth grade is a coach.
He wants to Go Go Go Go—
He wants to Get There!—and gives me a punch.
His wife, in lime slacks, curls on the couch.

I ask him where
and thinking it over he pounds his palm; his eyes stare.
His wife passes peanuts, teases
his touchy hair.

He says never mind
and changes the subject to button-hooks, quick dives
—old numbers in our pimples we were famous for.
Nineteen years go by; he calls it a crime.

His wife cracks two more Buds, stretches, calls it
a night; we hear the door click.
Flushed, he flicks on the television . . .
We bend our beer cans like dummies, and sit.

Gary Gildner

Football

The Game was ended, and the noise at last had died away, and now they gathered up the boys where they in pieces lay. And one was hammered in the ground by many a jolt and jar; some fragments never have been found, they flew away so far. They found a stack of tawny hair, some fourteen cubits high; it was the half-back, lying there, where he had crawled to die. They placed the pieces on a door, and from the crimson field, that hero then they gently bore, like soldier on his shield. The surgeon toiled the livelong night above the gory wreck; he got the ribs adjusted right, the wishbone and the neck. He soldered on the ears and toes, and got the spine in place, and fixed a gutta-percha nose upon the mangled face. And then he washed his hands and said: "I'm glad that task is done!" The half-back raised his fractured head, and cried: "I call this fun!"

Walt Mason

Bull-Dog!

Bull-dog! Bull-dog! Bow, wow, wow, Eli Yale,
Bull-dog! Bull-dog! Bow, wow, wow, Our team can never fail,
When the sons of Eli break thro' the line,
That is the sign we hail,
Bull-dog! Bull-dog! Bow, wow, wow, Eli Yale.

Cole Porter

Soccer at the Meadowlands

Near the goal, head sunk into his shoulders
  as he sprints, Chinaglia takes the ball
    spat at his feet,

dribbles it around a thatch of yellow shirts
  and, sliding between the legs
    of two defenders, belts it hard

into that caged, invisible *something*
  beyond the green reason of the field,
    in the netted calm no one enters.

The home crowd's ear-splitting rant
  grows seismic. Screams blur
    to wind howl and cymbals.

A jig-step. Chinaglia raises his fists
  as laurels. In a waking faint,
    he gallops round the pitch,

leaping, as if lovesick,
  into Marinho's arms, leaping
    to the hypnotic boom of the crowd.

Diane Ackerman

There's This That I Like about Hockey, My Lad

There's this that I like about hockey, my lad;
    It's a clattering, battering sport.
As a popular pastime it isn't half bad
    For chaps of the sturdier sort.
You step on the gas and you let in the clutch;
You start on a skate and come back on a crutch;
Your chance of surviving is really not much;
    It's something like storming a fort.

There's this that I like about hockey, my boy;
    There's nothing about it that's tame.
The whistle is blown and the players deploy;
    They start in to maul and to maim.
There's a dash at the goal and a crash on the ice;
The left wing goes down when you've swatted him twice;
And your teeth by a stick are removed in a trice;
    It's really a rollicking game.

There's this that I like about hockey, old chap;
    I think you'll agree that I'm right,
Although you may get an occasional rap,
    There's always good fun in the fight.
So toss in the puck, for the players are set,
Sing ho! for the dash on the enemy net;
And ho! for the smash as the challenge is met;
    And hey! for a glorious night!

John Kieran

Hockey

The ice is smooth, smooth, smooth.
The air bites to the center
Of warmth and flesh, and I whirl.
It begins in a game . . .
The puck swims, skims, veers,
Goes leading my vision
Beyond the chasing reach of my stick.

The air is sharp, steel-sharp.
I suck needles of breathing,
And feel the players converge.
It grows to a science . . .
We clot, break, drive,
Electrons in motion
In the magnetic pull of the puck.

The play is fast, fierce, tense.
Sticks click and snap like teeth
Of wolves on the scent of a prey.
It ends in the kill . . .
I am one of the pack in a mad,
Taut leap of desperation
In the wild, slashing drive for the goal.

Scott Blaine

Anthem

America, if you were a basketball court,
I'd double dribble down
all your edges. America, if you were a
basketball court, I'd take my shots
in every State. I'd begin with a foul
in Chicago, a set shot in Florida, a hook
in Alabama, and a jump shot in Washington.
O, America, I'd put hoops on all your edges,
backboards against every border and sea.
America I would elbow across country kicking
my feet up and over every player in sight. America,
I'd give you naked cheer leaders, electric bands
and Referees guided by the strings
that hang down from the Justice of Heaven. America,
I'd name everybody as my players. The teams
would be bi-sexual and place women in the spring
of every step. We'd move so fast you wouldn't be able
to count the colors of our players. There would be such
    rhythm
that the governor of every State would have to hide
in his box seat. The rafters would be loaded with lightning,
magnifying and giving life to each move, each pleasure.
We'd make this country move like a cyclone in heaven,
the star white twirl of our ankles
would crack and clear
the trance of Death. Nevada and Virginia would be the locker
    rooms
out of which we would come storming with our underground
    passions.
We'd have the tip-off in Kansas while the rooters swayed
to the rhythm of the Wizard of Oz, the fingers of the centers
    touching
and turning the ball like the small eye
of the Gulf's tornado. On defense, we'd move from State to
    State,

keeping our hands moving like quick birds
or breezes that tickle the slim stalks of wheat. On offense,
our bodies would move like ploughs insistent on breaking
the hard, spring ground. A chest pass over Nebraska,
fast breaks that we could steer through either Texas or
    Montana
quick little lay-ups through Oregon and Idaho, or little
    Vermont
and Maine. A bounce pass through Oklahoma and Tennessee.
    Faking,
moving, stopping, elbowing, quick as possible, deft as
both the sparrow and the hawk, pressing our feet against the
    floor,
bringing our arms up, springing as high as we can, letting the
    ball leave
our finger tips in a high, slim arch, watching it slip through a
    dark rim
into the white strings
and out of the new net. It would be a great game. Children
    would be born
from the depths of our springs. A fall away jump shot would
    yield
to the embrace of mothers. The long overhead pass from one
    end
of the court to the other would provoke
a family reunion. O, America, the land of the living,
the land of the dead, the land of our yet unknown gods
would be revealed through the terrible precision
of each of our moves. America, our heels charged with
    lightning,
our toes with sparks, we'd get all your States to nourish
each and every rooter. Loaves of bread and fish
would be on every corner. Your tired brown bleachers would
    be turned
into all colors of the rainbow. America, America,

if you were a basketball court and this brought us so close
to Heaven, when the Game was over, the sweat glimmering
        down
our silver spun bodies, America, we'd all slow down
and, as a finish to our efforts
we'd bring Mick Jagger in,
and watch him dance, move and sing,
and, as the white lights
went out, putting our arms
around each other, we'd watch him
take a fine, straw broom
and begin to gracefully sweep
the whale hearts
off the whole length of the floor.

   Stephen Vincent

Song: Take Who Takes You

Ice Man, Magic, Bird and McAdoo
Cliff, Kevin, Jamie and Lou
In the real world
just like the schoolyard game:
You Take Who Takes You

Somedays no way they're gonna fall
Play good D and move the ball
in the real world,
just like the schoolyard game:
don't call every call

Any pick-up game I ever been to
any pick-up scene of any kind
you will find they're easy to get into
if you only bear in mind that

You take who takes you
it's a basic principle and true
in the real world,
just like in the schoolyard game:
You take who takes you

No, me and my old lady, Heaven knows
It was a good match-up I suppose
But in the real world,
just like the schoolyard game:
It's good if it goes

    (Oh no it ain't)

It's good if it goes

    (Oh no it ain't)

IT'S GOOD IF IT GOES!

       Fred Gardner

(80)

Lanky Hank Farrow

What can you do when you're six five
but be on the basketball team—
dribble and drive in and pivot
and put it over the rim.

You get to think you're a big shot,
a lot of girls think so, too,
but after your senior year's finished
all you are is you—

and now you sit on the sidelines
forever out of the action.
Dad's given me a job
with Farrow and Briggs Construction

but grabbing the ball on the rebound,
leaping and tipping it in
while the crowd and the girls with the pompoms
go wild—never again.

Harold Witt

Nothing but Net

The jump shot? It's all in the wrist
and follow-through, and the timing
of the jump. Of course it's one thing
to hit one in a game of HORSE,
and something else over a guy
that's guarding you. What I like best
is shooting baskets by myself,
warming up gradually until,
at the very height of my jump,
I can tell that it's going in
as the ball leaves my fingertips,
arcing to intercept the air
at the dead center of the goal—
that one split second of eclipse.

Roy Scheele

Makin' Jump Shots

He waltzes into the lane
'cross the free-throw line,
fakes a drive, pivots,
floats from the asphalt turf
in an arc of black light,
and sinks two into the chains.

One on one he fakes
down the main, passes
into the free lane
and hits the chains.

A sniff in the fallen air—
he stuffs it through the chains
riding high:
"traveling" someone calls—
and he laughs, stepping
to a silent beat, gliding
as he sinks two into the chains.

Michael S. Harper

Point Guard.

You bring the ball down the court.

The pick is set.

The play is set. The movement of

the ball

is faster

than all

the

defensive

hands and heads,

and you

get free.

You pass into the big girl

at the key. She turns

and

shoots and scores.

The crowd roars.

Arnold Adoff

Fast Break

In Memory of Dennis Turner, 1946–1984

A hook shot kisses the rim and
hangs there, helplessly, but doesn't drop

and for once our gangly starting center
boxes out his man and times his jump

perfectly, gathering the orange leather
from the air like a cherished possession

and spinning around to throw a strike
to the outlet who is already shoveling

an underhand pass toward the other guard
scissoring past a flat-footed defender

who looks stunned and nailed to the floor
in the wrong direction, turning to catch sight

of a high, gliding dribble and a man
letting the play develop in front of him

in slow motion, almost exactly
like a coach's drawing on the blackboard,

both forwards racing down the court
the way that forwards should, fanning out

and filling the lanes in tandem, moving
together as brothers passing the ball

between them without a dribble, without
a single bounce hitting the hardwood

until the guard finally lunges out
and commits to the wrong man

(85)

while the power-forward explodes past them
in a fury, taking the ball into the air

by himself now and laying it gently
against the glass for a layup,

but losing his balance in the process,
inexplicably falling, hitting the floor

with a wild, headlong motion
for the game he loved like a country

and swiveling back to see an orange blur
floating perfectly through the net.

Edward Hirsch

Ex-basketball Player

Pearl Avenue runs past the high-school lot,
Bends with the trolley tracks, and stops, cut off
Before it has a chance to go two blocks,
At Colonel McComsky Plaza. Berth's Garage
Is on the corner facing west, and there,
Most days, you'll find Flick Webb, who helps Berth out.

Flick stands tall among the idiot pumps—
Five on a side, the old bubble-head style,
Their rubber elbows hanging loose and low.
One's nostrils are two S's, and his eyes
An E and O. And one is squat, without
A head at all—more of a football type.

Once Flick played for the high-school team, the Wizards.
He was good: in fact, the best. In '46,
He bucketed three hundred ninety points,
A county record still. The ball loved Flick.
I saw him rack up thirty-eight of forty
In one home game. His hands were like wild birds.

He never learned a trade, he just sells gas,
Checks oil, and changes flats. Once in a while,
As a gag, he dribbles an inner tube,
But most of us remember anyway.
His hands are fine and nervous on the lug wrench.
It makes no difference to the lug wrench, though.

Off work, he hangs around Mae's Luncheonette.
Grease-gray and kind of coiled, he plays pinball,
Sips lemon cokes, and smokes those thin cigars;
Flick seldom speaks to Mae, just sits and nods
Beyond her face towards bright applauding tiers
Of Necco Wafers, Nibs, and Juju Beads.

John Updike

Basketball: A Retrospective

My ethics were
    a good pair of hands,
     a good move
when things were difficult.

An exceptional man
    could change direction
     in the air,
could thread a needle.

Stephen Dunn

The Volleyball Match

Now we gathered for the match
Near muscle beach about 9 a.m.
My Dad was 34 or so, at peak form
Playing with Andy Aiken, who was tall
& heavy, but as useful to Jack Pearlman
As was the girl to "our hero" who made the
Challenge: "500 bucks me & a gal can beat you (Andy)
& anyone you can find." They didn't have a chance,
Jack put Andy down the line, covered
The entire court himself, and amazed
The gallery with leaps & digs &
Unreachable shots.
                    Walking back to the car
          I was proud & happy, Dad
                         Handed me 20 bucks out
                                  Of his joy

Bill Pearlman

Led by the Hebrew School Rabbi

Those good students who only loved working
through pages of exercises,
but were too good to object to the philanthropy
of physical recreation took a bus
to the Grand Concourse and another one down it,
modelled after the Champs Elysees in Paris, France,
to the aging YMHA by Yankee Stadium.

We stumbled on the basketball court
of that cavernous decrepit building
flapping like ducks, but outran the Yeshiva boys
whose tzitzis, even to us, were ridiculous,
a sign of obvious distress and incompetence.

In the pool, girls and boys segregated
across the Olympic length,
we didn't know what to do.
Nothing we could figure out.
Confused. Nothing we could read.
In rubber caps we floated and ducked,
white knots of feathers drifting in the musty steam.

Judith Baumel

"It's Great When You Get In"

They told me the water was lovely,
　That I ought to go for a swim,
The air was maybe a trifle cool,
　"You won't mind it when you get in."
So I journeyed cheerfully beach-ward,
　And nobody put me wise,
But everyone boosted my courage
　With an earful of jovial lies.

The Sound looked cold and clammy,
　The water seemed chilly and gray,
But I hastened into my bathing suit
　And floundered into the spray.
Believe me, the moment I touched it
　I realized then and there,
That the fretful sea was not meant for me
　But fixed for a polar bear.

I didn't swim for distance
　I didn't do the crawl,
(They asked why I failed to reach the raft,
　And I told them to hire a hall.)
But I girded my icy garments
　Round my quaking limbs so blue,
And I beat it back to the bath house
　To warm up for an age or two.

I felt like a frozen mummy
　In an icy winding sheet.
It took me over an hour
　To calm my chattering teeth.
And I sympathized with Peary,
　I wept for Amundsen's woes,
As I tried to awaken some life in
　My still unconscious toes.

So be warned by my example
   And shun the flowing sea,
When the chill winds of September
   Blow sad and drearily.
Heed not the tempters' chatter
   Pass them the skeptics' grin
For the greatest bull that a boob can pull
   Is "It's great when you get in."

Eugene O'Neill

The Lifeguard

In a stable of boats I lie still,
From all sleeping children hidden.
The leap of a fish from its shadow
Makes the whole lake instantly tremble.
With my foot on the water, I feel
The moon outside

Take on the utmost of its power.
I rise and go out through the boats.
I set my broad sole upon silver,
On the skin of the sky, on the moonlight,
Stepping outward from earth onto water
In quest of the miracle

This village of children believed
That I could perform as I dived
For one who had sunk from my sight.
I saw his cropped haircut go under.
I leapt, and my steep body flashed
Once, in the sun.

Dark drew all the light from my eyes.
Like a man who explores his death
By the pull of his slow-moving shoulders,
I hung head down in the cold,
Wide-eyed, contained, and alone
Among the weeds.

And my fingertips turned into stone
From clutching immovable blackness.
Time after time I leapt upward
Exploding in breath, and fell back
From the change in the children's faces
At my defeat.

Beneath them I swam to the boathouse
With only my life in my arms
To wait for the lake to shine back
At the risen moon with such power
That my steps on the light of the ripples
Might be sustained.

Beneath me is nothing but brightness
Like the ghost of a snowfield in summer.
As I move toward the center of the lake,
Which is also the center of the moon,
I am thinking of how I may be
The savior of one

Who has already died in my care.
The dark trees fade from around me.
The moon's dust hovers together.
I call softly out, and the child's
Voice answers through blinding water.
Patiently, slowly,

He rises, dilating to break
The surface of stone with his forehead.
He is one I do not remember
Having ever seen in his life.
The ground I stand on is trembling
Upon his smile.

I wash the black mud from my hands.
On a light given off by the grave
I kneel in the quick of the moon
At the heart of a distant forest
And hold in my arms a child
Of water, water, water.

James Dickey

400-Meter Freestyle

The gun full swing the swimmer catapults and
    cracks

                              s

                              i

                            x

feet away onto that perfect glass he catches at

a

n

  d

throws behind him scoop after scoop cunningly
    moving

                            t

                             h

                            e

water back to move him forward. Thrift is his
    wonderful

  s

e

  c

ret; he has schooled out all extravagance. No muscle

                              r

                              i

                            p

ples without compensation wrist cock to heel snap to

h

i

  s

mobile mouth that siphons in the air that nurtures

                              h

                            i

                            m

at half an inch above sea level so to speak.

T
h
e
astonishing whites of the soles of his feet rise
                                    a
                                        n
                                        d
salute us on the turns. He flips, converts, and is gone
a
l
 l
in one. We watch him for signs. His arms are steady
    at
                                            t
                                                h
                                                e
catch, his cadent feet tick in the stretch, they know
t
h
e
lesson well. Lungs know, too; he does not list for
                                        a
                                        i
                                        r
he drives along on little sips carefully expended
b
u
t
that plum red heart pumps hard cries hurt how soon
                                            i
                                                t
                                                s
near one more and makes its final surge

TIME: 4:25:9

Maxine Kumin

(96)

Medals and Money: A Re-evaluation

i loved swimming until it became a nightmare for
me until it turned into a fear trip
when i became a winner afraid to lose
because america can't love a loser,
a second-place person

i loved the thrill of international competition
until nationalism and commercialism
and finally murder itself
causes me to re-evaluate why

why i ever wanted to win
in the first place

just what are we winning
if the costs are so high
a loss of identity,
a loss of self
a loss of soul
a sacrifice to the gold
gold gold and more gold

my god, where have our values gone
that a fellow athlete swimmer
after brilliantly coming back from his defeat in '68
to victory in '72
has to cash in for the pictures

drink-milk signs make me puke

sports is dying
how you play the game means nothing
it's winning and how many and how much
it's me me me me me
as it has to be if you want to win
but at what price winning?

every waking hour in the pool to get better to win more
to dedicate yourself so much to one thing
that you block out the rest of life

when to take time to take a walk
a park
the sea
a kiss
to fight to free the athletes from their ridiculous rules
is it all medals and money, america?

where is the soul of sports

american sports scene filled with racism and sexism
corrupt and greedy lying lustful people
who are doing it in the name of the athlete
in the name of the country
in the name of the all-american way
gone mad.

it's time to get it all out and look at it
a good long hard look
at what we have become in american sports
now another battleground for pent-up hate
and frustrations
where backroom decisions and confused officials
bloody the sports world just as
surely as the gun
the athlete is the political hostage here, now

he works hard to win
the coach is dedicated and tries to help him
both have desire to please each other

all athletes strive for the best they can put out
why then should seven be more important than one
gold medal
in the long run
who cares how many

no more heroes please
no more gods to live up to and worship

can't we do it for the fun of it,
for the love of it
instead of the gold of it

can't we get off the teat of the sacred cow,
the false idol
and into what it's really all about,

love

doing it
for the love of it

Barbara Lamblin

The Bathers

Man and woman, they enter the sea,
The animal-blue, the bovine slippery wave
That, rising, bares its corrugations
And, falling, takes them in its silky teeth
Tightly, while the vast body mills around
Their already watery bodies, till, half blind,
They pass invisibly through its bony sheath,
Swallowed alive and gasping and let go.

They do not even hear the crash of it
Behind them, where it wrecks itself on land,
But are already willed by water,
Weightless and far gone in forgetfulness.

And they are born in that unrisen sky
Out there where all is bright and water-galled
And the loose guts of water tangle them
And then dissolve; where only the dead wave
Comes back awhile, dissipated
And scattered on the wide wash of the sea.

The bathers, blissful in primeval tears,
Forgotten even by the sea itself
That rocks them absently, two bobbing heads,
Onions or oranges
Dumped by the freight of summer on the sea.

They lose even the power of speech;
They must go back to learn;
They make the difficult return
Where nets of water hold them, feel their legs,
Cast ropes of coldness round their bellies,
Trip them, throw gravel at their ankles,

Until, unpredictably, the entire sea
Makes them a path and gives them a push to the beach.
And they lie down between the yellow boats
Where the sun comes and picks them out
And rubs its fire into their sea-pale flesh,
Rubbing their blood, licking their heavy hair,
Breathing upon their words with drying fire.

Karl Shapiro

The Nude Swim

On the southwest side of Capri
we found a little unknown grotto
where no people were and we
entered it completely
and let our bodies lose all
their loneliness.

All the fish in us
had escaped for a minute.
The real fish did not mind.
We did not disturb their personal life.
We calmly trailed over them
and under them, shedding
air bubbles, little white
balloons that drifted up
into the sun by the boat
where the Italian boatman slept
with his hat over his face.

Water so clear you could
read a book through it.
Water so buoyant you could
float on your elbow.
I lay on it as on a divan.
I lay on it just like
Matisse's *Red Odalisque*.
Water was my strange flower.
One must picture a woman
without a toga or a scarf
on a couch as deep as a tomb.

The walls of that grotto
were everycolor blue and
you said, "Look! Your eyes
are seacolor. Look! Your eyes
are skycolor." And my eyes
shut down as if they were
suddenly ashamed.

Anne Sexton

Swimming in the Pacific

At sunset my foot outreached the mounting Pacific's
Last swirl as tide climbed, and I stood
On the mile-empty beach backed by dune-lands. Turned,
    saw,
Beyond knotting fog-clots, how Chinaward now
The sun, a dirty pink smudge, grew larger, smokier,
More flattened, then sank.

Through sand yet sun-hot, I made to my landmark—
Gray cairn to guard duck pants (not white now), old drawers,
Old sneakers, T-shirt, my wallet (no treasure).
At dune-foot I dressed,
Eyes westward, sea graying, one gull at
Great height, but not white-bright, the last
Smudge of sun being gone.

So I stood, and I thought how my years, a thin trickle
Of sand grains—years I then could
Count on few as fingers and toes—had led me
Again and again to this lonesome spot where
The sea might, in mania, howl, or calm, lure me out
Till the dunes were profiled in a cloud-pale line,
Nothing more,
Though the westering sun lured me on.

But beachward by dusk, drawn back
By the suction of years yet to come—
So dressed now, I wandered the sand, drifting on
Toward lights, now new, of the city afar, and pondered
The vague name of Time,
That trickles like sand through fingers,
And is life.

But suppose, after sorrow and joy, after all
Love and hate, excitement and roaming, failure, success,
And years that had long trickled past
And now could certainly never
Be counted on fingers and toes—suppose
I should rise from the sea as of old
In my twilit nakedness,
Find my cairn, find my clothes, and in gathering fog,
Move toward the lights of the city of men,
What answer, at last,
Could I give my old question? Unless,
When the fog closed in,
I simply lay down, on the sand supine, and up
Into grayness stared and, staring,

Could see your face, slow, take shape.

Like a dream all years had moved to.

Robert Penn Warren

Surfers at Santa Cruz

They have come by carloads
with Styrofoam surfboards
in the black wetsuits
of the affluent sixties,
the young Americans

kneeling paddle with their palms
and stand through the breakers
One World Polynesians
lying offshore
as if they were fishing for the village.

They are waiting for the ninth wave
when each lone boy falling downhill
ahead of the cresting hundreds of yards
balancing communicates
with the ocean on the Way

how beautiful they are
their youth and human skill
and communion with the nature of things,
how ugly they are
already sleek with narrow eyes.

Paul Goodman

Fancy Dive

The fanciest dive that ever was dove
Was done by Melissa of Coconut Grove
She bounced on the board and flew in the air
With a twist of her head and a twirl of her hair
She did thirty-four jackknives, backflipped and spun,
Quadruple gainered and reached for the sun
And then somersaulted nine times and a quarter
And looked down and saw that the pool had no water.

Shel Silverstein

The Springboard

Like divers, we ourselves must make the jump
That sets the taut board bounding underfoot
Clean as an axe blade driven in a stump;
But afterward what makes the body shoot
Into its pure and irresistible curve
Is of a force beyond all bodily powers.
So action takes velocity with a verve
Swifter, more sure than any will of ours.

Adrienne Rich

Haiti: Skin Diving

My legs break
the thick glass floor
of water.

My foot magnifies
blue as the foot
of a corpse.

One unshuttable eye
spans my face
and sees easily

what two eyes
can hardly see.
I breathe

and go under.
Sea urchins fan
black sprays of quills.

Sea fans sway
at right angles
to the current.

My snorkel's ball
spins in its atmopshere
of breath

like tiny Mars
above my head.
The sixth sense

must be gravity!
I measure distance
now by fin-kicks,

by the sun's angle.
Finned, the swimmer
wades backwards

to the sea,
waist-deep, to plunge
and turn almost

weightless inside
the moving
body once again.

All the lyre-tailed,
stippled, rainbow-
flecked bodies

flash—shaped by water.
A school of fish
spills from the coral

and circles me.
I stiffen
without moving.

My fingertip's
slightest tremor
could shatter that order,

blurring
as my breath
clouds the mask.

Jane Shore

The Skydivers

This is a fervent time
    for flying.
        Do not foul
        my fall in a fit
  of wing-waggling!
  Hold
  steady
  as
  we
  touch.
  The
  force
  of
  flight
  tears
  away
  all
  sham.
  Enter
  upon
  the
  wind's
  fingers.
  H
  o
  o
  o
  o
  l
  d
  !
  m
  e
  e
  e
  e
  !

Joseph Colin Murphy

(111)

Hazard's Optimism

Harnessed and zipped on a bright
October day, having lied to his wife,
Hazard jumps, and the silk spanks
open, and he is falling safely.

This is what for two years now
he has been painting, in a child's palette
—not the plotted landscape that holds dim
below him, but the human figure dangling safe,
guyed to something silky, hanging here,
full of half-remembered instruction
but falling, and safe.

They must have caught and spanked him
like this when he first fell.
He passes it along now, Hazard's vision.
He is in charge of morale in a morbid time.
He calls out to the sky, his voice
the voice of an animal that makes not words
but a happy incorrigible noise, not
of this time. The colors of autumn
are becoming audible through the haze.

It does not matter that the great masters
could see this without flight, while
dull Hazard must be taken up again and dropped.
He sees it. Then he sees himself
as he would look from the canopy above him,
closing safely (if he can remember
what to do) on the Brueghel landscape.
Inside the bug-like goggles, his eyes water.

William Meredith

The Skaters

Black swallows swooping or gliding
In a flurry of entangled loops and curves,
The skaters skim over the frozen river.
And the grinding click of their skates as they impinge upon
    the surface,
Is like the brushing together of thin wing-tips of silver.

John Gould Fletcher

Skate

Off-
balance, into the wide wide world
she's going to wow
on one foot:
she always does things the hard way. Down
of course, her mother imagines
her long bones breaking, her long
convalescence.
          No harm done. It's twilight
there's music, a woman
holding her daughter's shoes in her lap
and the ice almost exactly the color of medals.
But not yet.

Laurel Blossom

To Kate, Skating Better Than Her Date

Wait, Kate! You skate at such a rate
You leave behind your skating mate.
Your splendid speed won't you abate?
He's lagging far behind you, Kate.
He brought you on this skating date
His shy affection thus to state,
But you on skating concentrate
And leave him with a woeful weight
Pressed on his heart. Oh, what a state
A man gets into, how irate
He's bound to be with life and fate
If, when he tries to promulgate
His love, the loved one turns to skate
Far, far ahead to demonstrate
Superior speed and skill. Oh, hate
Is sure to come of love, dear Kate,
If you so treat your skating mate.
Turn again, Kate, or simply wait
Until he comes, then him berate
(Coyly) for catching up so late.
For, Kate, he *knows* your skating's great,
He's *seen* your splendid figure eight,
He is not here to contemplate
Your supersonic skating rate—
That is not why he made the date.
He's anxious to expatiate
On how he wants you for his mate.
And don't you want to hear him, Kate?

David Daiches

(115)

Skater in Blue

The lid broke, and suddenly the child
in all her innocence was underneath
the ice in zero water, growing wild
with numbness and with fear. The child fell
so gently through the ice that none could tell
at first that she was gone. They skated on
without the backward looks that might have saved
her when she slipped, feet first, beneath the glaze.
She saw the sun distorted by the haze
of river ice, a splay of light, a lost
imperfect kingdom. Fallen out of sight,
she found a blue and simple, solid night.
It never came to her that no one knew
how far from them she'd fallen or how blue
her world had grown so quickly, at such cost.

Jay Parini

Skaters

There are many tonight and the rink
is like a Brueghel, such motion
and animation, at first glance
some busy microcosm.

Above the rink I lean on the rail,
my sleeve settling in the residue
of sticky drink and on the rail
beside it, scratched: *Letitia*

loves Spud. Below, the skaters
circle crazily, looking now like
a swarm but soon you begin
to see that two types stand out:

The helpless scarecrows so tenuous
and bad they command the attention
they fear—you can almost hear
them pray for balance.

The others you notice of course
circle with such skill they seem
to fly. They skate with their hands
behind their backs and show

enormous deference by giving the inept
berths wide enough for ships.
In truth they're in their element,
a kind of royalty down there

but so good that they're benign.
Like royalty they know they need
the awkward to set them off.
One cuts an elaborate figure

of concern for a fallen child
showing he's not only good on skates
but good at heart. Another averts
what we're meant to believe

is a disaster with arms thrown up
and a nifty shift when a scarecrow
falls twenty feet away.
                              Thinking
of Letitia and Spud who were moved

to pledge their love right here, I realize
the Brueghel swirl below just may be
a little version of the world. Though
all the gestures seem too large,

like a silent movie—mimed
danger and concern, pratfalls,
the rubber-kneed drunks, bad
music in the background,

and love pledged in the balcony.

Vern Rutsala

Skating in Pleasant Hill, Ohio

I flew past Theising's Drug Store
wishing I had a nickel for ice-cream,

past Charlie's who fixed cars and everyone's problems,
who couldn't fix things the day nephew Crissy died
and we cried by the gas pumps.

I flew past Klopfer's where I'd go for bubble gum
or a sucker when I was four and had one penny.

I could never decide so Mr. Klopfer would say,
"Here, Sweetie, you just take both."

I'd race toward the only hill in our village,
the one that went straight down to the cemetery.

Once you started, there was no stopping
until you reached the big iron gate.

Breathless, I'd look through to the tombstones,
watch Mr. Lavey scything weeds.

We took flowers for Grandma on Memorial Day,
"Have a little respect," Dad would hiss
and yank us off a mound of grass.

If I rested too long at the gate, Mr. Lavey would ask,
"Want to come in?"

I'd say, "Not today, Mr. Lavey,"
unstrap my skates
and scramble back up the hill.

Kathleen Iddings

The Sidewalk Racer

OR

On the Skateboard

    Skimming
  an asphalt sea
I swerve, I curve, I
sway; I speed to whirring
sound an inch above the
ground; I'm the sailor
and the sail, I'm the
driver and the wheel
I'm the one and only
    single engine
     human auto
      mobile.

Lillian Morrison

Remembering You

Skiing the mountain alone
on a day of difficult moods
with snowflakes of rottenstone
at the liverish altitudes

and the bones of the birches pale
as milk and the humpbacked spine
of an untouched downhill trail
turned suddenly serpentine,

a day comes into my head
when we rose by aerial tram,
bubbles strung on a thread
of a mobile diagram,

rose to the mountain's crest
on a day of electric blue
and how, my enthusiast,
I made the descent with you,

the beautiful greed of our run
taken on edge, tiptoe
with a generous spill of sun
on the toytown roofs below

as on powder side by side
running lightly and well
we lipped and took the untried,
easily parallel.

Maxine Kumin

Ski Song of the U.S. Army's Tenth Mountain Division

Men of steel and sons of Mars,
Under freedom's stripes and stars.
We are ski men,
We are free men,
And mountains are our home.
White-clad G.I. Joe,
We're the Phantoms of the Snow,
On our ski-boards we're the mountain infantry,
Happy-go-lucky; free.
And from Kiska to the Alps,
Where the wind howls thru our scalps,
With a slap slap slap
Of a pack against our back,
We will bushwhack on to victory!

W. T. Levitt

International Ski-Flying Championship, Obersdorf

Protected by thick brick walls
and the fire on the hearth
I watch a man slide
down the white
roller-coaster slope

over the jump and
soar into the sky
body parallel to skis
skis perpendicular to snow
way down below—

O Icarus, if you had only known!
All that fuss with feathers and wax!
What you really needed were
two skinny wood slats
and snow on those brown Greek hills.

I know it's hot in this room
but a man has flown
523 feet
without motor and wings
and I am shivering.

Elisavietta Ritchie

Sailing, Sailing

Lines written to keep the mind off incipient seasickness

There is no impeding
That proceeding,
No deflating
That undulating
Or overthrowing
The to-and-froing
Or undoing
The fro-and-toing,
That silky insisting
Never desisting,
That creasing, uncreasing
Never ceasing,
No deterrence
To the recurrence,
No cessation
To the pulsation,
No stopping the dropping
Of the wave,
The plopping, slopping
Of the foam.
We brave it
Afloat in a boat
On the perpetual
Wet-you-all
(No controlling that rolling)
Motion
Hasten, Jason
Of the ocean.
Get the basin.

Lillian Morrison

Yacht for Sale

My youth is
Made fast
To the dock
At Marseilles
Rotting away
With a chain to her mast,

She that saw slaughters
In foreign waters:

She that was torn
With the winds off the Horn:

She that was beached in the bleaching environs
Of sirens:

She that rounded the Cape of Good Hope
With a rope's aid:

She's fast there
Off the Cannebiere.

It's easy to see
She was frail in the knee
And too sharp in the bow—
You can see now.

Archibald MacLeish

Choosing Craft

Striped equilateral sails,
the morning placid,
corners tugged trim,
jab for the belly of the wind.
Try to be accurate.
One tall, white isosceles spanks water,
helped by outboard motor,
canvas popping in a made breeze.
Put forth without effort.
Then expect, what neither gust
nor inertia will upset, to upset.
Let the wind pick up.
Tricorn scraps, as for a chance-built
quilt over the cove, scoot free.
How close-hauled, canted, apt to capsize
you keep, must be why you don't.

May Swenson

Eight Oars and a Coxswain

Eight oars compel
Our darting shell,
Eight oar-blades flash the sun;
The hard arms thrill,
The deep lungs fill,
Eight backs are bent as one.
All silver lined
We leave behind
Each wave of somber hue.
"Stroke! Stroke!
Stroke! Stroke!
Steady, Number Two!"

The sea-gulls go,
A drift of snow,
On Hudson's lights and shades;
The eagle swings
On splendid wings
Above the Palisades.
Let caution steer
The shore anear,
But Valor takes the tide.
"Stroke! Stroke
Stroke! Stroke!
Ease your forward slide!"

A fair league still
To old Cock Hill,
Where Spuyten Duyvil roars.
No time for play!
Give 'way; give 'way!
And bend the driven oars!

When breezes blow
Then feather low
With level blades and true.
"Stroke! Stroke!
Stroke! Stroke!
Steady! Pull it thr-o-o-ough!"

Arthur Guiterman

Caught

I stand beside the sea and cast.

I feel a nibble. At last

He swallows the hook and takes out line.

Quick ratchet; reel him in, he's mine!

Gaston Dubois

Out Fishing

We went out, early one morning,
Over the loud marches of the sea,
In our walnut-shell boat,
Tip-tilting over that blue vacancy.

Combering, coming in,
The waves shellacked us, left us breathless, ill;
Hour on hour, out
Of this emptiness no fish rose, until

The great one struck that twine-
Wrapped flying-fish hard, turned and bolted
Off through the swelling sea
By a twist of his shoulder, with me tied fast; my rod

Held him, his look held me,
In tug-of-war—sidesaddle on the ocean
I rode out the flaring waves,
Rode till the great fish sounded; by his submersion

He snapped the line, we lost
All contact; north, south, west, my adversary
Storms on through his world
Of water: I do not know him: he does not know me.

Barbara Howes

The Fish

I caught a tremendous fish
and held him beside the boat
half out of water, with my hook
fast in a corner of his mouth.
He didn't fight.
He hadn't fought at all.
He hung a grunting weight,
battered and venerable
and homely. Here and there
his brown skin hung in strips
like ancient wall paper,
and its pattern of darker brown
was like wall paper:
shapes like full-blown roses
stained and lost through age.
He was speckled with barnacles,
fine rosettes of lime,
and infested
with tiny white sea-lice,
and underneath two or three
rags of green weed hung down.
While his gills were breathing in
the terrible oxygen
—the frightening gills
fresh and crisp with blood,
that can cut so badly—
I thought of the coarse white flesh
packed in like feathers,
the big bones and the little bones,

the dramatic reds and blacks
of his shiny entrails,
and the pink swim-bladder
like a big peony.

I looked into his eyes
which were far larger than mine
but shallower, and yellowed,
the irises backed and packed
with tarnished tinfoil
seen through the lenses
of old scratched isinglass.
They shifted a little, but not
to return my stare.
—It was more like the tipping
of an object toward the light.
I admired his sullen face,
the mechanism of his jaw,
and then I saw
that from his lower lip
—if you could call it a lip—
grim, wet, and weapon-like,
hung five old pieces of fish-line,
or four and a wire leader
with the swivel still attached,
with all their five big hooks
grown firmly in his mouth.
A green line, frayed at the end
where he broke it, two heavier lines,
and a fine black thread
still crimped from the strain and snap
when it broke and he got away.
Like medals with their ribbons
frayed and wavering,
a five-haired beard of wisdom
trailing from his aching jaw.

I stared and stared
and victory filled up
the little rented boat,
from the pool of bilge
where oil had spread a rainbow
around the rusted engine
to the boiler rusted orange
the sun-cracked thwarts,
the oarlocks on their strings,
the gunnels—until everything
was rainbow, rainbow, rainbow!
And I let the fish go.

Elizabeth Bishop

Fish Story

All the fishermen here remember the one
about the man found dead in a drifting boat
with a one hundred seventy-five pound halibut.
In its thrashing it had knocked him
against a thwart and beaten him to death.
Dangerous to bring those things aboard.
Best to shoot them in the head first
or hook them with a flying gaff and tow them.

Alone once on the Strait of Juan De Fuca
I had one tow *me* in my boat for over an hour
before the line broke.
I had to imagine thirty fathoms deep
that great flat strength rising like
a section of the ocean floor to inhale my bait.

Henry Carlile

Salmon-Fishing

The days shorten, the south blows wide for showers now,
The south wind shouts to the rivers,
The rivers open their mouths and the salt salmon
Race up into the freshet.
In Christmas month against the smoulder and menace
Of a long angry sundown
Red ash of the dark solstice, you see the anglers,
Pitiful, cruel, primeval,
Like the priests of the people that built Stonehenge,
Dark silent forms, performing
Remote solemnities in the red shallows
Of the river's mouth at the year's turn,
Drawing landward their live bullion, the bloody mouths
And scales full of the sunset
Twitch on the rocks, no more to wander at will
The wild Pacific pasture nor wanton and spawning
Race up into fresh water.

Robinson Jeffers

The Pike

The river turns,
Leaving a place for the eye to rest,
A furred, a rocky pool,
A bottom of water.

The crabs tilt and eat, leisurely,
And the small fish lie, without shadow, motionless,
Or drift lazily in and out of the weeds.
The bottom-stones shimmer back their irregular striations,
And the half-sunken branch bends away from the gazer's eye.

A scene for the self to abjure!—
And I lean, almost into the water,
My eye always beyond the surface reflection;
I lean, and love these manifold shapes,
Until, out from a dark cove,
From beyond the end of a mossy log,
With one sinuous ripple, then a rush,
A thrashing-up of the whole pool,
The pike strikes.

Theodore Roethke

The Catch

Happy to have these fish!
In spite of the rain, they came
to the surface and took
the No. 14 Black Mosquito.
He had to concentrate,
close everything else out
for a change. His old life,
which he carried around
like a pack. And the new one,
that one too. Time and again
he made what he felt were the most
intimate of human movements.
Strained his heart to see
the difference between a raindrop
and a brook trout. Later,
walking across the wet field
to the car. Watching
the wind change the aspen trees.
He abandoned everyone
he once loved.

Raymond Carver

Ice-Fishing

The men cut windows into ice
looking for fish below winter's cover.
The sky, stretched over the trees,
holds back the snow's descent
with its pale blue skin.

Below, the fish sway, like drunkards.
Cold lake water, pressed under the ice,
presses their fins stiff.

The men let down their lines.
Their hooks break forth like falling stars,
flashing before the fish's eyes
coaxing them into another world
where fish dangle from the hook,
snapping their tails, uselessly, in air.

Hours later a thin glaze
steals over the old fishing holes.
A young child returns
to try her foot in the line's descent,
shattering what fragile ice
had grown back there.

Her blood slows in her red boot,
like the fish's slow swishing fins,
Ice forms in layers between stock and flesh.

Denise Pendleton

Hunting

In Harry's Discounts Men & Boys
red and redandblack hunter's caps
pop up in rows like ducks. The boy
grown so fast his soft bones show
gazes over the edges of the red rows.

His father hovers, darts from jackets to caps
to socks, not quite looking at the boy,
his low edgy voice repeating:
Pick the ones you really want.
Let me show you some I like, to give
you an idea, he says, moving toward
a rack of boots. Picking out a pair,
half turning, quietly: You still like
the Winchester? More'n the Savage?

Leaning close to hear they catch
themselves before they touch, freeze
the space between them. Then the boy
slowly lets go his breath, reaches out
to feel the boots his father hands him.

Jack Sheedy

The Rabbit-Hunter

Careless and still
The hunter lurks
With gun depressed,
Facing alone
The alder swamps
Ghastly snow-white.
And his hound works
In the offing there
Like one possessed,
And yelps delight
And sings and romps,
Bringing him on
The shadowy hare
For him to rend
And deal a death
That he nor it
(Nor I) have wit
To comprehend.

Robert Frost

Nine Charms against the Hunter

In the last bar on the way to your wild game,
May the last beer tilt you over among friends
And keep you there till sundown—failing that,
A breakdown on the road, ditching you gently
Where you may hunt for lights and a telephone.
Or may your smell go everywhere through the brush,
Upwind or crosswind. May your feet come down
Invariably crunching loudly on dry sticks.
Or may whatever crosses your hairlines—
The flank of elk or moose, the scut of a deer,
The blurring haunch of a bear, or another hunter
Gaping along his sights at the likes of you—
May they catch you napping or freeze you with buck fever.
Or if you fire, may the stock butting your shoulder
Knock you awake around your bones as you miss,
Or then and there, may the noise pour through your mind
Imaginary deaths to redden your daydreams:
Dazed animals sprawling forward on dead leaves,
Thrashing and kicking, spilling themselves as long
As you could wish, as hard, as game,
And then, if you need it, imaginary skinning,
Plucking of liver and lights, unraveling guts,
Beheading trophies to your heart's content.
Or if these charms have failed and the death is real,
May it fatten you, hour by hour, for the trapped hunter
Whose dull knife beats the inside of your chest.

David Wagoner

Idyll

Within a quad of aging brick,
Behind the warty warden oak,
The Radcliffe sophomores exchange,
In fencing costume, stroke for stroke;
Their bare knees bent, the darlings duel
Like daughters of Dumas and Scott.
Their sneakered feet torment the lawn,
Their skirted derrières stick out.

Beneath the branches, needles glint
Unevenly in dappled sun
As shadowplay and swordplay are
In no time knitted into one;
The metal twitters, girl hacks girl,
Their educated faces caged.
The fake felt hearts and pointless foils
Contain an oddly actual rage.

John Updike

The Need to Win

When an archer is shooting for nothing
He has all his skill.
If he shoots for a brass buckle
He is already nervous.
If he shoots for a prize of gold
He goes blind
Or sees two targets—
He is out of his mind!

His skill has not changed. But the prize
Divides him. He cares.
He thinks more of winning
Than of shooting—
And the need to win
Drains him of power.

Thomas Merton

Black Lady in an Afro Hairdo
Cheers for Cassius

Honey-hued beauty, you are:
in your gleaming white shorts,
gladiator shoes,
sparkling robe of satin cream,
bursting through the ropes,
piercing the arena smoke
with your confident eyes
of Kentucky brown.
Only *now* do I realize
what it must have been like
to have known Sweet Sugar
when he was King,
or to have prayed for Joe
when the ear of the ghetto
was pressed hard
to the sound machine.
But what you bring
to the ring, no
black champ has
ever brought before—
Sweet Cassius,
you are *my* pride
in these times of pain;
fast moving,
grooving in the ring
with that pepped-up cat
who acts so bold.
Child, your hands so fast
you make the young seem old!
So, mock him once or twice
for me, baby.
Sting him 'side the head,
spin, cool Daddy,
to the side.

Ease up a bit now
and let the man ride.
Now, in the eye—
jab, jab,
Ali Shuffle,
Ooh, heavens!!
The dude is down—
Did you see it?

R. Ernest Holmes

They All Must Fall

They all must fall
In the round I call.

Muhammad Ali

Shadowboxing

Sometimes you almost get a punch in.
Then you may go for days without even seeing him,
or his presence may become a comfort
for a while.

He says: I saw you scrambling last night
on your knees and hands.

He says: How come you always want to be
something else, how come you never take your life
seriously?

And you say: Shut up! Isn't it enough
I say I love you, I give you everything!

He moves across the room with his hand
on his chin, and says: How great you are!

Come here, let me touch you, you say.

He comes closer. Come closer, you say.
He comes closer. Then. *Whack!* And
you start again, moving around and around
the room, the room which grows larger
and larger, darker and darker. The black moon.

James Tate

The Loser

and the next I remembered I'm on a table,
everybody's gone: the head of bravery
under light, scowling, flailing me down . . .
and then some toad stood there, smoking a cigar:
"Kid you're no fighter," he told me,
and I got up and knocked him over a chair;
it was like a scene in a movie, and
he stayed there on his big rump and said
over and over: "Jesus, Jesus, whatsamatta wit
you?" and I got up and dressed,
the tape still on my hands, and when I got home
I tore the tape off my hands and
wrote my first poem,
and I've been fighting
ever since.

Charles Bukowski

The Seventh Round

Give it to him!
To you, they mean.
As always (mezzanine
Gone dazzling dim,

A crown at stake)
Before you stands
The giver with clenched hands.
Drop your own. Take.

James Merrill

The Boxing Match

Am I really a sports fan, I ask myself,
listening to the Dempsey-Firpo fight
over the radio and looking
at the open mouths of my friends:
Dempsey has just knocked Firpo out
of the ring, I am somewhat apathetic;
I can observe myself being surprised
but all the others are yelling with delight.
Of course I'm a sports fan, I assure myself.
Dempsey knocking Firpo out of the ring
is something I couldn't do. I could admit
that and admire strength. I fear it also
and I look around again and think
how if I scoffed at this hullabaloo
about a man being knocked out of the ring
these boys would turn on me and knock me down,
and I join in the yelling. Firpo
is climbing back into the ring
and I am glad for him
and admire him.

David Ignatow

Young Wrestlers

The beautiful boys curve and writhe,
gone inward behind their contorted masks.
The blind hands reach;
the legs hook, lock, lever
the gleaming bodies into hold,
out of hold. Escape. Riding time.
"Sink a half!" and the arm snakes
rapid with love around the neck.

One is left who will cry somewhere.
For the other, the air bends
in to him, hot with voices.
The walls reappear, the colors.
He is one body again,
lonely with joy.
Many sweet dreams will be based
on that ferocious touch.

Grace Butcher

Wrestling The Beast.

This guy is an animal. A pig?   Squealing sinus breathing.

A bear?   Hair on his fat arms.

A dog?   No, not biting, but his

chin

digging into my collar

bone.

A dragon. Easy. Dragon breath.

An anaconda snake. His mistake:

choke hold around my neck.

A jackal? A hyena? A hungry lion?

A wounded tiger

alone in the dark bush?

A bee?

An

ant? A worm? A toad? A dying fly on the end of a frog's

tongue?

This guy is an animal. A gentle cat rolled

         over

   by me.

   O n e.

   T w o.

   Three.

Arnold Adoff

Karate

If I could chop wood.
if I could just cut through
this furniture.

the paraphernalia
of blocks
and stacks of boards,
wedged and
piled
head-high,

if I could break the back
of a single two-by-four,

if the Japanese instructor would only
lay his little building
of bricks
in front of me,

if I could only drive nails
deep into the hard rose of the wood.

Stanley Plumly

Pumping Iron

She doesn't want
the bunchy look
of male lifters:
torso an unyielding love-knot,
arms hard at mid-boil.
Doesn't want
the dancing bicepses
of pros.
Just to run her flesh
up the flagpole
of her body,
to pull her roaming flab
into tighter cascades,
machete a waist
through the jungle
of her hips,
a trim waist
two hands might grip
as a bouquet.

Diane Ackerman

My Father Toured the South

My father and his muscles
toured the South posing
in store windows stripped down
past his biceps. He was young then,
dark eyes like dates, hair
like a black sandbar. Full of rush
to crush cities and worlds
like the air he shushed off
when he brought the loose strap up
round his chest and inhaled
till he filled it, proving
the power of physical culture.

When I was nine and he in the forties
I found his pictures, profiled in tights
like a small John L. He laughed
when I showed them, and with a thumb
in his mouth blew up his arm
like an auto tire we tried
to squeeze down and couldn't.

Now that proud and laughing strength
folds to a memory of store windows
and caught ohs from his children's lips
as he hefted us up to the ceiling
and swung us back like easy dumbbells.
His arms are half-caste traitors to a wish
with no more weights to lift,
nothing his youth need move by muscle,
no cities to push flat for the sake
of proving strength. Only the muscles in his head
still flex and dance as his arms did once
in that old thumb game and the strap
across his brain pulls tight again and again.

Jeannette Nichols

Women's Tug of War at Lough Arrow

In a borrowed field they dig in their feet
and clasp the rope. Balanced
against neighboring women, they hold
the ground by the little gained
and leaning like boatmen rowing into
the damp earth, they pull
to themselves the invisible waves, waters
overcalmed by desertion
or the narrow look trained to a brow.

The steady rain has made girls of them,
their hair in ringlets. Now they haul
the live weight to the cries
of husbands and children, until the rope
runs slack, runs free
and all are bound again by the arms
of those who held them, not until, but so
they gave.

Tess Gallagher

Unsound Condition

They're checking the Ping-Pong ball,
For something, it seems, is wrong.
It pongs when it ought to ping
And it pings when it ought to pong.

Richard Armour

Preparedness

When you've had yourself accoutered
   In the finest tennis clothes
And been sedulously tutored
   By the best of tennis pros
And have spent long hours choosing
   Among racquets by the score
And have sat up nights perusing
   All the books of tennis lore
And have studied drop-shot placement
   With devotion that appalls
And worked weekends in your basement
   With a Thing that belches balls
And developed comprehension
   Of the principles of Zen
To make sure that tennis tension
   Won't disrupt your game again
And grown thoroughly familiar
   With the art of gamesmanship—
You'll be feeling that much sillier
   When you lose the set six-zip.

Felicia Lamport

The Tennis

Circled by trees, ringed with the faded folding chairs,
The court awaits the finalists on this September day,
A peaceful level patch, a small precise green pool
In a chrysanthemum wood, where the air smells of grapes.
Someone has brought a table for the silver cup.
Someone has swept the tapes. The net is low;
Racket is placed on racket for the stretch.
Dogs are the first arrivals, loving society,
To roll and wrestle on the sidelines through the match.
Children arrive on bicycles. Cars drift and die, murmuring.
Doors crunch. The languorous happy people stroll and wave,
Slowly arrange themselves and greet the players.
Here, in this unpretentious glade, everyone knows everyone.
And now the play. The ball utters its pugging sound:
Pug pug, pug pug—commas in the long sentence
Of the summer's end, slowing the syntax of the dying year.
Love-thirty. Fifteen-thirty. Fault.
The umpire sits his highchair like a solemn babe.
Voices are low—the children have been briefed on etiquette;
They do not call and shout. Even the dogs know where to
    stop,
And all is mannerly and well behaved, a sweet, still day.
What is the power of this bland American scene
To claim, as it does, the heart? What is this sudden
Access of love for the rich overcast of fall?
Is it the remembered Saturdays of "no school"—
All those old Saturdays of freedom and reprieve?
It strikes as quickly at my heart as when the contemptuous
    jay
Slashes the silence with his jagged cry.

E. B. White

The Midnight Tennis Match

Note. In midnight tennis each player gets three serves
rather than the usual two.

You are tired
of this maudlin country club
and you are tired of his insults.
You'd like to pummel his forehead
with a Schweppes bottle
in the sauna, but instead
you agree, this time,
to meet him at midnight
on the tennis court.

When you get there
you can't see him
but you know he is waiting
on the other side of the net.
You consider briefly
his reputation.

You have first serve
so you run toward the net
and dive over it.
You land hard on your face.
It's not a good serve: looking up
you can barely see his white shorts
gleam in the darkness.

You get up, go back
to your side of the net
and dive over again.
This time you slide
to within a few feet of him.
Now you can make out his ankles
the glint of the moon
and his white socks.

Your last serve is the best:
your chin stops one inch
from the tip of his sneakers.
Pinheads of blood
bloom across your chest.
You feel good crawling
back to your side again.

Now it is his turn
and as he runs toward the net
you know he's the fastest man
you've ever seen.

His dive is of course flawless.
He soars by you,
goes completely off the court
and onto the lawn,
demolishing a few lounge chairs.
To finish, he slides
brilliantly onto the veranda.

You go up and sit beside him
and somehow
you don't feel too humiliated:
he is still unconscious.
At least now you know why
he is undefeated. It's
his sensitive, yet brutal, contempt.
With a similar contempt
you pour a gallon of water on his face.
He still has two more serves—

Thomas Lux

Tennis in the City

for Arthur Ashe

He could help us out
selling papers or sacking groceries
but that's what I did growing up.
Every day he's in the alley
knocking that ball against the building.
Whomp   take that   Forest Hills
whomp   whomp   take that   Wimbledon
whomp   whomp   whomp
all   day   long,
the wife tells me so.
Says she watches him from the window
when the bossman has her clean 'em,
says she doesn't know about that boy.
But I know about that boy
and I know this ball's worn
and I know this racket's gonna split
no matter how much tape you put on,
so tonight after supper
we're going for new ones, son.
And I want you to start staying
in that alley an hour longer, hear?

Frank Higgins

A History of Golf—Sort Of

*More than 500 years ago in Scotland, men became so distracted by
the game of golf that they were neglecting archery and other military
activities. So, starting in 1457, three successive Scottish kings pro-
hibited golf. But the fourth king, James IV, became an avid golfer.*

On Scotland's rolling highlands in
   The fifteenth century,
The Scots were playing golf; a change
   From their barbarity.

But not for long. The game was banned
   By three old-fashioned kings.
The Scots returned to archery
   And other warlike things.

Then James the Fourth assumed the throne,
   And he took up the game.
He liked it. As an honor, they
   Immortalized his name.

From tee to green throughout the world,
   Thenceforth and evermore,
When golfers go around the course,
   You'll hear them holler, "IV!"

Thomas L. Hirsch

A Lesson from Golf

He couldn't use his driver any better on the tee
Than the chap that he was licking, who just happened to be
    me;
I could hit them with a brassie just as straight and just as far,
But I piled up several sevens while he made a few in par;
And he trimmed me to a finish, and I know the reason why:
He could keep his temper better when he dubbed a shot
    than I.

His mashie stroke is choppy, without any follow through;
I doubt if he will ever, on a short hole, cop a two,
But his putts are straight and deadly, and he doesn't even
    frown
When he's tried to hole a long one and just fails to get it
    down.
On the fourteenth green I faded; there he put me on the
    shelf,
And it's not to his discredit when I say I licked myself.

He never whined or whimpered when a shot of his went
    wrong;
Never kicked about his troubles, but just plodded right along.
When he flubbed an easy iron, though I knew that he was
    vexed,
He merely shrugged his shoulders, and then coolly played the
    next,
While I flew into a frenzy over every dub I made
And was loud in my complaining at the dismal game I played.

Golf is like the game of living; it will show up what you are;
If you take your troubles badly you will never play to par.
You may be a fine performer when your skies are bright and
    blue
But disaster is the acid that shall prove the worth of you;
So just meet your disappointments with a cheery sort of grin,
For the man who keeps his temper is the man that's sure to
    win.

      Edgar Guest

(165)

First Green Heron

I wouldn't have seen her,
if I hadn't been in the rough
searching for a plugged ball

near the frog pond that guards
the green, trapping all the willow
dust. But looking for something

else is when you find what is
there, what the branches and leaves
hold as their own, until danger

passes, here, meaning to hit out
of trouble, move on to the next
hole. Looking down, I wouldn't

have thought to look up, especially
in this place where the first unwritten
rule is Keep your head down. Though

something must have told me there's
more nearby that's afraid than meets
the eye. I don't know what I saw

first, my ball buried in the unforgiving
muck or her, who I couldn't take my eye
off once I knew she was there, once

she moved out of the picture that hid
her, held her identical to a life
she could become when someone swung

too near, because they had forgotten
the second rule of a good swing,
Swing easy and don't try to kill it.

Gary Margolis

Genuine Poem, Found on a Blackboard in a Bowling Alley in Story City, Iowa

If you strike
when head pin
is red pin,
one free game
to each line.
Notify desk
before you throw
if head pin
is red

Ted Kooser

Hook

My father limps on the leg that healed short.
His twice-broken right wrist, too weak to hold
a bowling ball palm up, is why he spins
a hook he cannot control. The ball rolls
slowly, as if limping while it wanders
from one gutter to the other and back.

We stand dead last in the Father and Son
League, not helped by my rocketing straight shots
that knock down nothing as often as they
knock down everything. He watches, giving
no advice. At thirteen, knowing there is
nothing for me to say either, I wait

for the ball's return so I can heft it
again and aim down the gleaming alley.

Floyd Skloot

Clean

Break, kid. You get one chance.
Not quite.
Three in the corner. That camper
out there's mine, red truck with the cap.
Seven, one rail, cross side-pocket.
Left Biloxi six this morning.
Five'll kiss the thirteen, corner.
Thought I'd come track down a beer.
Yeah?
Long green, one'll drop, far corner.
Bought that truck last year—old man died.
Split the two four, two in the side.
Cashed his policy and I'm set.
Six up and back. It's been eight months
on the road. Four off the fifteen.
I guess I've got enough to drive
till I die. Eight in the corner,
clean.
     Name's Mickey. Budweiser, please.

Lance Newman

The Gymnasts

Legs v-ed out from the groin's nugget
—the many figured as a single man.
Or the milling centipede of crossed purposes
pulling itself together and rising
from the ground up, in honor of itself.
And not to form the structures only, but
to be present in the flesh and confirmed
by others present equally to them
—leaving as early almost as the sun,
they come down from separate rooms, starting
from Elizabeth or Hoboken or the Bronx,
walking on their hands among us now
or spelling out with their spinning persons
leaping sentences of cartwheels and vaults.
Nearby, the body-builders are defining
their "pecs," biceps, "glutes"—glowing maps
of somber worlds in single display,
so distant that they sink slowly
into the background of every sky.
But here the gymnasts build themselves
together, embody what they illustrate:
serenity of power in action, strength
moving in matters of common concern;
and, by wall or mound or pyramid,
by honeycomb, womb, huddle, swarm
and tower—these sociable forms, forms
of habitation—in the middle of nowhere
bestow a sense to everything.

Irving Feldman

Un*e*v*e*n Para llel Bars

Twisting
      swing
           a

  moment of flight

and catch
        Around

and turn
           the floor

the ceiling
    Hands and the Bar

Pausing

     Spinning fury squeezed into a pose
     Bursting almost before it is held

Circle
   and

Twist
   Swing
       and release

Hands
    poised
    in the instant of waiting

          Eternity
          before

the Catch.

      Patricia Gary

(171)

The Runner

On a flat road runs the well-trained runner,
He is lean and sinewy with muscular legs,
He is thinly clothed, he leans forward as he runs,
With lightly closed fists and arms partially raised.

Walt Whitman

Morning Athletes

for Gloria Nardin Watts

Most mornings we go running side by side
two women in mid-lives jogging, awkward
in our baggy improvisations, two
bundles of rejects from the thrift shop.
Men in their zippy outfits run in packs
on the road where we park, meet
like lovers on the wood's edge and walk
sedately around the corner out of sight
to our own hardened clay road, High Toss.

Slowly we shuffle, serious, panting
but talking as we trot, our old honorable
wounds in knee and back and ankle paining
us, short, fleshy, dark haired, Italian
and Jew, with our full breasts carefully
confined. We are rich earthy cooks
both of us and the flesh we are working
off was put on with grave pleasure. We
appreciate each other's cooking, each
other's art, photographer and poet, jogging
in the chill and wet and green, in the blaze
of young sun, talking over our work,
our plans, our men, our ideas, watching
each other like a pot that might boil dry
for that sign of too harsh fatigue.

It is not the running I love, thump
thump with my leaden feet that only
infrequently are winged and prancing,
but the light that glints off the cattails

(173)

as the wind furrows them, the rum cherries
reddening leaf and fruit, the way the pines
blacken the sunlight on their bristles,
the hawk circling, stooping, floating
low over beige grasses,
                                    and your company
as we trot, two friendly dogs leaving
tracks in the sand. The geese call
on the river wandering lost in sedges
and we talk and pant, pant and talk
in the morning early and busy together.

Marge Piercy

His Running My Running

Mid-autumn late autumn
At dayfall in leaf-fall
A runner comes running.

How easy his striding
How light his footfall
His bare legs gleaming.

Alone he emerges
Emerges and passes
Alone, sufficient.

When autumn was early
Two runners came running
Striding together

Shoulder to shoulder
Pacing each other
A perfect pairing.

Out of leaves falling
Over leaves fallen
A runner comes running

Aware of no watcher
His loneness my loneness
His running my running.

Robert Francis

Birthday on the Beach

At another year
I would not boggle,
Except that when I jog
I joggle.

Ogden Nash

The Photograph

I promised to take your picture
the day you ran
in the 10,000 meter race
sponsored by the local bank.
I studied the route
and picked the best spot
vowing to watch like a prize-winning journalist
or the wife of an astronaut
for you to run by.
The background:
houses near a school,
oak trees in autumn.
Call it pastoral verging on urban,
picturesque enough
to appear to make sense
as the fleetest of runners appeared
on the street cleared of cars.

At first there was only a trickle,
runners in town for the weekend,
national favorites come to inspire the local joggers,
those who had made it a hobby or a career or a compulsion,
jogging bums,
and those who represented tennis shoe makers
or a general line of sporting equipment.
I did not expect you there.
Then the runners came thicker.
Many wore commemorative t-shirts
from other such races,
the Butte to Butte Rally,
the Over-the-Hill 10,000,
the big one in Boston,
but still I didn't see you.

Could there really be so many,
had jogging undone so many?
Like the plagues of Shelley's autumn.
Had you fallen by the way?

I held my camera ready
and tried to frame the scene
of agonizing faces,
of red and sweating faces,
the pumping legs,
the working arms,
the pain,
but tears came up in my eyes.
It was like a Japanese monster movie
when the crowd flees through the city.
It was six o'clock television
and a mob surrounding the embassy.
It was a platinum print of a ballroom
with European ladies and gentlemen
dancing and having a good time
just before the start of World War I.

What's the point in a race
where the runners are forty abreast?
My camera fell on its strap
and dangled against my chest.
A siren wailed.
I would never find you.

Then all of a sudden, movement,
like a trout in a fast stream,
like the first pulse
in the primordial soup,
a leaping in front of me,
your arms waving,
your voice shouting,
"I'm here," "I'm here," and "I'm here,"

as I snapped your picture,
front, side, and backside
and you ran on to finish,
neither first nor last but middle.
Then I laughed and walked to the finish
to join you in celebration,
and safe in the camera your picture
was leaping and shouting, "I'm here!"

Barbara Drake

Strategy for a Marathon

I will start
when the gun goes off.
I will run
for five miles.
Feeling good,
I will run
to the tenth mile.
At the tenth
I will say,
"Only three more
to the halfway."
At the halfway mark,
13.1 miles,
I will know
fifteen is in reach.
At fifteen miles
I will say,
"You've run twenty before,
keep going."
At twenty
I will say,
"Run home."

Marnie Mueller

The Finish

The first runner reached us
bearing the news before
he was expected by
the camera crews—the instant
replay showed him strolling
by the roadside, sucking
half an orange. Who'd think
he had endured so many
miles? They demanded
he re-run the final
fifty yards while they
re-filmed him. While they filmed him
a second runner crossed
the line but by the time
the cameras turned to him
the second runner wasn't
running any longer
but sucking half an orange;
he too must re-enact
the second finish, since
the public is entitled
to the real thing.
Just as he re-crossed
the line, finishing second
a second time, here comes
puffing up the hill
the third man, at his heels
the crazy crowd the first
runner came to tell of
but had no chance to tell
anyone while cameras
caught his second first
finish and then turned
from him and scanned the second

finish of the second
finisher, the spent
third man with an orange
in his hand, the raggle-
taggle mob arriving
at the reviewing stand,
and soon there's blood all over
the finish line and no
reviewers and no stand,
but what viewer could
believe this, cameras still
following the third
man suck his orange? The crews
urge the crowd once more
to re-enact the finish—

Daniel Hoffman

Interview with a Winner

What was it like?
like losing
same bloody feet
blazing tendons
same sweet release
melancholia of exhaustion

What did you win?
a chance

For what?
to do it again
that wasn't it
either

What did you get?
through

What's left for you?
tomorrow's race

losing is worse

Donald Finkle

Running

1933 (North Caldwell, New Jersey)

What were we playing? Was it prisoner's base?
I ran with whacking keds
Down the cart-road past Rickard's place,
And where it dropped beside the tractor-sheds

Leapt out into the air above a blurred
Terrain, through jolted light,
Took two hard lopes, and at the third
Spanked off a hummock-side exactly right,

And made the turn, and with delighted strain
Sprinted across the flat
By the bull-pen, and up the lane.
Thinking of happiness, I think of that.

Richard Wilbur

Hurdler

He quickly steps over the air,
bends at the barriers
in the wind of his own speed.
Only a certain rhythm
flattens the strange stair:
the lean tall galloping,
the certain foot slashing away
the layered backdrop
up the incline
of the slanted air.

Grace Butcher

Pole Vaulter

The approach to the bar
is everything

unless I have counted
my steps   hit my markers
feel up to it   I refuse
to follow through
I am committed to beginnings
or to nothing

planting the pole
at runway's end
jolts me to my task
out of sprinting
I take off   kicking in
and up   my whole weight
trying the frailty
of fiberglass

never forcing myself
trusting it is right
to be taken to the end
of tension   poised for
the powerful thrust to
fly me beyond expectation

near the peak
I roll my thighs inward
arch my back   clearing
as much of the bar as I can
(knowing the best jump
can be cancelled
by a careless elbow)

and open my hands

David Allan Evans

The Standing Broad Jump

Good at something, I practiced till I broke
the record by a foot. And then they said
forget it. "Think you're a grasshopper?
We haven't done that trick for twenty years."

Champion of the obsolete event,
I hook my toes on the board, spring forth,
and, just as I would fall, throw back my arms
and fly my whole ten feet to the measured sand.

Richard Frost

The Racer's Widow

The elements have merged into solicitude.
Spasms of violets rise above the mud
And weed, and soon the birds and ancients
Will be starting to arrive, bereaving points
South. But never mind. It is not painful to discuss
His death. I have been primed for this—
For separation—for so long. But still his face assaults
Me; I can hear that car career again, the crowd coagulate on
    asphalt
In my sleep. And watching him, I feel my legs like snow
That let him finally let him go
As he lies draining there. And see
How even he did not get to keep that lovely body.

Louise Glück

Motorcycle Racer Thinks of Quitting

Fear is a golden chain around my throat,
fastening me to this motorcycle,
this fine fierce animal that is a threat
to my very being, would as soon kill
me as caress these thighs I hug it with.
It leaps low along gray rivers of sound,
granting me my paradoxical wish.
How beautiful the fear has always seemed.

But each lap, in some other dimension,
holds empty spaces that all go nowhere.
The rider, crashing, falling into one,
does not come around again. Is not there.

Fear grows more bright and golden as I ride;
I am almost too dazzled to decide.

Grace Butcher

Riding Lesson

I learned two things
from an early riding teacher.
He held a nervous filly
in one hand and gestured
with the other, saying, "Listen.
Keep one leg on one side,
the other leg on the other side,
and your mind in the middle."

He turned and mounted.
She took two steps, then left
the ground, I thought for good.
But she came down hard, humped
her back, swallowed her neck,
and threw her rider as you'd
throw a rock. He rose, brushed
his pants and caught his breath,
and said, "See, that's the way
to do it. When you see
they're gonna throw you, get off."

Henry Taylor

Billy Could Ride

I

Billy was born for a horse's back!—
That's what Grandfather used to say:—
He'd seen him in dresses, a-many a day,
On a two-year-old, in the old barn-lot,
Prancing around, with the bridle slack,
And his two little sunburnt legs outshot
So straight from the saddle-seat you'd swear
A spirit-level had plumbed him there!
And all the neighbors that passed the place
Would just haul up in the road and stare
To see the little chap's father boost
The boy up there on his favorite roost,
To canter off, with a laughing face.—
Put him up there, he was satisfied—
And O the way that Billy could ride!

I I

At celebration or barbecue—
And Billy, a boy of fifteen years—
Couldn't he cut his didoes there?—
What else would you expect him to,
On his little mettlesome chestnut mare,
With her slender neck, and her pointed ears,
And the four little devilish hooves of hers?
The "delegation" moved too slow
For the time that Billy wanted to go!
And to see him dashing out of the line
At the edge of the road and down the side
Of the long procession, all laws defied,

And the fife and drums, was a sight divine
To the girls, in their white-and-spangled pride,
Wearily waving their scarfs about
In the great "Big Wagon," all gilt without
And jolt within, as they lumbered on
Into the town where Billy had gone
An hour ahead, like a knightly guide—
O but the way that Billy could ride!

I I I

"Billy can ride! Oh, Billy can ride!
But what on earth can he do beside?"
That's what the farmers used to say,
As time went by a year at a stride,
And Billy was twenty if he was a day!
And many a wise old father's foot
Was put right down where it should be put,
While many a dutiful daughter sighed
In vain for one more glorious ride
With the gallant Billy, who none the less
Smiled at the old man's selfishness
And kissed his daughter, and rode away,—
Touched his horse in the flank—and *zipp!*—
Talk about horses and horsemanship!—
Folks stared after him just wild-eyed. . . .
Oomh! the way that Billy could ride!

James Whitcomb Riley

Horseback

for Raymond Carver

Never afraid of those huge creatures
I sat sky-high on my western saddle
As we roared through the woods of skinny pine,
The clump clump of his great delicate hooves
Stirring up plumes of pine-needle dust,
One hand casual on the pommel,
The other plunged in the red coarse hair of his mane.

I recall the day he stopped dead on the trail
Trembling all over. We heard the chattering song
Of the rattler. My hypnotised bay
Couldn't move. Time stopped: The burnt odor of sage,
The smoky noon air, and the old old snake
As big around as my skinny wrist
Rising up from his rock.

Then the screen goes blank, and next it's summer camp:
I've conquered a wild mare, bare-back, whipping one arm
In sky-ward circles like a movie cowboy,
Screaming with joy.
So now when a stubborn skittery horse runs away with me
I give him his head. But as he tried to skin me off,
Plunging under low branches, I grit, "Oh no you don't!"

I bury my face in his neck, hang on for dear life,
Furious, happy, as he turns to race for home.
We pound into the stable yard and I dismount,
But wonder at curious glances turned my way
Until I see myself in the tack-room mirror,

My face a solid mass of purple welts.
Then I begin to sneeze and sneeze. My allergies
Burst into bloom, and I am forced to quit.
I don't sit a mount again for twenty years
Until I get to Pakistan
And Brigadier Effendi puts me up
On his perfect Arab mare.
My thighs tighten the old way as I marry a horse again . . .
I just wanted to tell you about it, Ray.

Carolyn Kizer

Stallion

A gigantic beauty of a stallion, fresh and responsive to my
    caresses,
Head high in the forehead, wide between the ears,
Limbs glossy and supple, tail dusting the ground,
Eyes full of sparkling wickedness, ears finely cut, flexibly
    moving.

His nostrils dilate as my heels embrace him,
His well-built limbs tremble with pleasure as we race around
    and return.
I but use you a minute, then I resign you, stallion.
Why do I need your paces when I myself out-gallop them?
Even as I stand or sit passing faster than you.

Walt Whitman

Polo Ponies Practicing

The constant cry against an old order,
An order constantly old,
Is itself old and stale.

Here is the world of a moment,
Fitted by men and horses
For hymns,

In a freshness of poetry by the sea,
In galloping hedges,
In thudding air:

Beyond any order,
Beyond any rebellion,
A brilliant air

On the flanks of horses,
On the clear grass,
On the shapes of the mind.

Wallace Stevens

Bronco Busting, Event #1

The stall so tight he can't raise heels or knees
when the cowboy, coccyx to bareback, touches down

tender as a deerfly, forks him, gripping the rope-
handle over the withers, testing the cinch,

as if hired to lift a cumbersome piece of brown
luggage, while assistants perched on the rails arrange

the kicker, a foam-rubber band around the narrowest,
most ticklish part of the loins, leaning full weight

on neck and rump to keep him throttled, this horse,
"Firecracker," jacked out of the box through the sprung

gate, in the same second raked both sides of the belly
by ratchets on booted heels, bursts into five-way

motion: bucks, pitches, swivels, humps, and twists,
an all-over-body-sneeze that must repeat

until the flapping bony lump attached to his spine is gone.
A horn squawks. From the dust gets up a buster named
    Tucson.

May Swenson

The Closing of the Rodeo

The lariat snaps; the cowboy rolls
  His pack, and mounts and rides away.
Back to the land the cowboy goes.

Plumes of smoke from the factory sway
  In the setting sun. The curtain falls,
A train in the darkness pulls away.

Good-by, says the rain on the iron roofs.
  Good-by, say the barber poles.
Dark drum the vanishing horses' hooves.

William Jay Smith

The Ball Poem

What is the boy now, who has lost his ball,
What, what is he to do? I saw it go
Merrily bouncing, down the street, and then
Merrily over—there it is in the water!
No use to say "Oh there are other balls":
An ultimate shaking grief fixes the boy
As he stands rigid, trembling, staring down
All his young days into the harbor where
His ball went. I would not intrude on him,
A dime, another ball, is worthless. Now
He senses first responsibility
In a world of possessions. People will take balls,
Balls will be lost always, little boy,
And no one buys a ball back. Money is external.
He is learning, well behind his desperate eyes,
The epistemology of loss, how to stand up
Knowing what every man must one day know
And most know many days, how to stand up.
And gradually light returns to the street,
A whistle blows, the ball is out of sight,
Soon part of me will explore the deep and dark
Floor of the harbor . . . I am everywhere,
I suffer and move, my mind and my heart move
With all that move me, under the water
Or whistling, I am not a little boy.

John Berryman

Nine Triads

Three grand arcs:
    the lift of the pole vaulter over the bar
    the golf ball's flight to the green
    the home run into the bleachers

Three pleasurable curves:
    the ice skater's figure eight
    the long cast of the fisherman
    the arched back of the gymnast

Three swishes that lift the heart:
    the basketball's spin through the net
    the skier's swoop down the snowpacked hill
    the diver's entry into the water

Three glides of satisfaction:
    the ice hockey forward's, after the goal
    the swimmer's turn at the end of the pool
    the finish of the bobsled run

Three swift arrivals to admire:
    the completed pass
    the arrow into the bull's-eye
    the sprinter at the tape

Three shots requiring skill:
    the slapshot
    the shot-put
    the putt-out

Three carriers of suspense:
    the place kick for a field goal
    the rim shot
    three balls and two strikes

Three vital sounds:
    the hunter's horn
    the starter's gun
    the bell for the end of the round

Three excellent wishes:
    to move the body with grace
    to fly without a machine
    to outrun time

Lillian Morrison

Among the Poets and Players

Robert Francis (p. 3) was a keen observer of male athletes. His many books of poetry are full of boys swimming, diving, wrestling, skiing, and playing baseball and other sports. . . . *Damon Runyon* covered sports for newspapers in the 1920s and 30s. In those days it was not uncommon for reporters to write poems as part of their sports coverage. *Babe Ruth* (p. 4) was thought by fans and reporters to have an ugly face and a peculiar style of running the bases. . . . Babe's Yankee teammate, *Lou Gehrig* (p. 5) died of a slow, wasting disease now known as Lou Gehrig's disease. . . . *Carl Hubbell* (p. 6) pitched for the baseball Giants before they moved from New York to San Francisco. . . . *Lucille Clifton* says of herself, "I am a black woman poet, and I sound like one." In her short, precise poem (p. 7) she *shows* us the entire career of *Jackie Robinson*, the first black player in the major leagues. . . . "Country" was the nickname of home-run hitter *Enos Slaughter* (p. 9). . . . Poets *Joel Oppenheimer* (p. 12) *and Tom Clark* (p. 14) have each published dozens of poems about baseball. . . . Many football fans consider *Vince Lombardi* (p. 15) to have been the greatest football coach ever. He led the Green Bay Packers to five NFL Championships and two Super Bowl wins. Poet *James Dickey* played football as a student at Clemson University. He describes his own coach there, Shag Norton, in another of his football poems, "The Bee." . . . Both *Johnny Unitas* (p. 18) and *Billy Ray Smith* (p. 19) played for the Baltimore Colts during the Colts' NFL Championship seasons. *Ogden Nash*, the most often-quoted of any modern American poet, wrote "My Colts," a series of poems about his favorite players. The series, illustrated with action photos, appeared in *Life* magazine. . . . *Big Daddy Lipscomb* (p. 20) also played for the Colts. . . . *Patrick Ewing* (p. 23) led his Georgetown University team to an NCAA championship. He was later the first-round draft pick of the New York Knicks. Ewing's fan, poet *Diane Ackerman*, is an athlete herself: a runner, scuba diver, and horsewoman. She tells about her experience learning to fly an airplane in her book *On Extended Wings*. . . . Norwegian *Sonja Henie* (p. 24) won three Olympic gold medals for figure skating, in 1928, 1932, and 1936. She moved to America to skate in films and in traveling ice shows that she organized and directed. . . . In the poem "Blues for Benny Kid Paret," (p. 25) *Dave Smith* writes about listening to the Championship fight in 1962 between Paret and Emile Griffith. Benny Paret was beaten so brutally he died ten days later. The beating reminds Smith of his own childhood encounter with a swarm of wasps. . . . Sports reporter *Grantland Rice* celebrates *Mildred "Babe" Didrikson* (p. 27), who won two gold medals and a silver at the 1932 Los Angeles Olympics. She gave up being a track and field athlete to become a golfer so that she could have a professional sports career in an age when few women had the chance to earn a living as an athlete. She won every major women's golf tournament, seventeen of them in a row during the 1940s. . . . Distance runner *Steve Prefontaine* (p. 29) died in a car accident before he fulfilled his promise as an international record breaker. Mystery surrounds the circumstances of the crash.

"Take Me Out to the Ball Game" (p. 31), written in the 1890s, is still the most popular song about baseball. . . . *Carl Sandburg* (p. 33) was one of the first poets to listen to the voices of his fellow Americans and set their common speech down in his poetry. . . . *Lillian Morrison* (p. 36) was for many years a young-adult librarian in New York City. She has written six books of poetry, which include more poems about sports than about any one other subject. . . . *Lawrence Ferlinghetti* believes that poets should write to arouse people. In "Baseball Canto" (p. 37) his passionate enthusiasm for Chicano and black players contrasts with the bland Anglo-Saxon poetry he's reading. For Ferlinghetti, the baseball diamond is free territory where anything can happen. . . . Twenty-eight poems about the mighty Casey can be found in *The Annotated Casey at the Bat* (University of Chicago Press). Two others besides "Casey's Daughter at the Bat" (p. 40) are about woman baseball players: "Mrs. Casey at the Bat" and "Casey's Sister at the Bat." Wife, sister, and daughter strike out. . . . His own childhood sports life is the frequent subject of poet *Gary Gildner* (p. 44). He has been poet-in-

residence at Reed College in Oregon and currently teaches poetry writing at Drake University. . . . *William Jay Smith* (p. 50) has published twenty volumes of poetry, including several for children. He says, "I believe poetry begins in childhood and that a poet who can remember his own childhood exactly can, and should, communicate to children." His light touch is at work in "World Champions." . . . Poet *Donald Hall* (p. 52) grew up hearing his grandfather reciting "Casey at the Bat" and other poems as they did their chores together on the family farm in New Hampshire. Hall is now a full-time writer. His forty-five books include a biography of former baseball star Dock Ellis. . . . Here is the answer key to the baseball poem "The Song of Snohomish" (p. 53):
The players' names, in order of appearance in the poem, are:

Catfish: George Metkovich; Mudcat: Jim Grant; Ducky: Joe Medwick; Coot: Orville Veale; The Babe: George Herman Ruth; The Barber: Salvatore Maglie; The Blade: Jack Billingham; The Brat: Eddie Stanky; Windy: John McCall; Dummy: William Hoy; Gabby: Charles Hartnett; Hoot: Walter Evers; Big Train: Walter Johnson; Big Six: Christy Mathewson; Big Ed: Edward Delehanty; Fat: Bob Fothergill.

Greasy: Alfred Neale; Sandy: Sanford Koufax; Muddy: Herold Ruel; Rocky: Rocco Colavito; Bunions: Rollie Zeider; Twinkle-toes: George Selkirk; Footsie: Wayne Belardi; The Hat: Harry Walker; Fuzzy: Al Smith; Dizzy: Jay Hanna Dean; Buddy: John Hassett; Cocky: Eddie Collins; The Bull: Al Ferrara; The Stork: George Theodore; The Weasel: Don Bessent; The Cat: Harry Brecheen.

Schoolboy: Lynwood Rowe; Preacher: Elwin Roe; Rajah: Rogers Hornsby; Duke: Edwin Snider; General: Alvin Crowder; Major: Ralph Houk; Spaceman: Bill Lee; Spook: Forrest Vandergrift Jacobs.

Shoeless Joe: Joseph Jefferson Jackson; Cobra Joe: Joe Frazier; Bullet Joe: Leslie Bush; Bing: Edmund Miller; Old Hoss: Charles Radbourne; Mule: George Haas; Country: Enos Slaughter; Rube: George Waddell; Smokey Joe: Joe Wood; Fireman Joe: Joe Beggs; Jersey Joe: Joe Stripp; Ping: Frank Bodie; Bull-dog: Jim Bouton; Squirrel: Roy Sievers; Puddin' Head: Willie Jones; Boob: Eric McNair.

The Georgia Peach: Ty Cobb; The Fordham Flash: Frank Frisch; The Flying Dutchman: Honus Wagner; Cot: Ellis Deal; The People's Cherce: Fred Walker; The Blazer: Wade Blassingame; Crash: Lawrence Davis; The Staten Island Scot: Bobby Thomson.

Skeeter: James Webb; Scooter: Phil Rizzuto; Pepper: Johnny Martin; Duster: Walter Mails; Ebba: Edward St. Claire; Bama: Carvel Rowell; Boomer: Ron Blomberg; Buster: Calvin Coolidge Julius Caesar Tuskahoma McLish.

Specs: George Toporcer; The Grey Eagle: Tris Speaker; The Toy Cannon: Jim Wynn; Tex: James Carleton; The Earl of Snohomish: Earl Averill; The Duke of Tralee: Roger Bresnahan; Art the Great: Arthur Shires; Gorgeous George: George Sisler; Ox: Oscar Eckhardt; Double X: Jimmie Foxx; The Nashville Narcissus: Charles Lucas; The Phantom: Julian Javier; The Flea: Freddie Patek.

The Little Professor: Dominic Paul DiMaggio; The Iron Horse: Lou Gehrig; Cap: Adran Anson; Iron Man: Joe McGinnity; Iron Mike: Mike Marshall; Iron Hands: Chuck Hiller; Hutch: Fred Hutchinson; Jap: William Barbeau; The Mad Russian: Lou Novikoff; Irish: Emil Meusel; Swede: Charles Risberg; Nap: Napoleon Lajoie; Germany: Herman Schaefer; Frenchy: Stanley Bordagaray; Big Serb: John Miljus; Dutch: Emil Leonard; Turk: Omar Lown; Tuck: George Stainback; Tug: Frank McGraw; Twig: Wayne Terwilliger; Spider: John Jorgensen; Birdie: George Tebbets; Rabbit: Walter Maranville; Pig: Frank House.

Three-Finger: Mordecai Peter Centennial Brown; No-Neck: Walt Williams; The Knuck: Hoyt Wilhelm; The Lip: Leo Durocher; Casey: Charles Dillon Stengel; Dazzy: Clarence Vance; Hippity: Johnny Hopp; Zim: Don Zimmer; Flit: Roger Cramer; Bad Henry: Henry Aaron; Fat Freddie: Frederick Fitzsimmons; Flip: Al Rosen; Jolly Cholly: Charles Grimm; Sunny Jim: James Bottomley.

Shag: Leon Chagnon; Schnozz: Ernesto Lombardi; King Kong: Charlie Keller; Klu: Ted Kluszewski; Boog: John Wesley Powell;

Buzz: Russell Arlett; Boots: Cletus Elwood Poffenberger; Bump: Irving Hadley; Boo: David Ferriss.

Baby Doll: William Jacobson; Angel Sleeves: Jack Jones; Pep: Lemuel Young; Sliding Billy: Billy Hamilton; Buttercup: Louis Dickerson; Bollicky: Billy Taylor; Boileryard: William Clarke; Juice: George Latham; Colby Jack: Jack Coombs; Dauntless Dave: Dave Danforth; Cheese: Albert Schweitzer; Gentle Willie: William Murphy; Trolley Line: Johnny Butler; Wagon Tongue: Bill Keister; Rough: Bill Carrigan; What's the Use: Pearce Chiles.

Ee-yah: Hugh Jennings; Poosh 'Em Up: Tony Lazzeri; Skoonj: Carl Furillo; Slats: Marty Marion; Ski: Oscar Melillo; Ding Dong: Bill Bell; Ding-a-Ling: Dain Clay; Dim Dom: Dominic Dallessandro; Dee: Wilson Miles.

Bubbles: Eugene Hargrave; Dimples: Clay Dalrymple; Cuddles: Clarence Marshall; Pinky: Mike Higgins; Poison Ivy: Ivy Paul Andrews; Vulture: Phil Regan; Stinky: Harry Davis.

Jigger: Arnold Statz; Jabbo: Ray Jablonski; Jolting Joe: Joseph Paul DiMaggio; Blue Moon: Johnny Lee Odom; Boom Boom: Walter Beck; Bubba: Wycliffe Nathaniel Morton; Bo: Robert Belinsky.

F. Scott Fitzgerald wrote "Football" (p. 57) when he was a fifteen-year-old student at Newman School. . . . *Ernest Hemingway* was also a student when he wrote "Dedicated to F.W." (p. 58) and published it in his Oak Park and River Forest High School newspaper. Hemingway co-wrote with a fellow student three other football poems. These and a baseball poem have been collected in his *88 Poems*. . . . *Mel Glenn* (p. 66) is a high-school teacher in Brooklyn, New York, who writes poems about his students. . . . *The Collected Poems of Howard Nemerov* won the Pulitzer Prize and the National Book Award in 1978. Nemerov is a professor of English at Washington University in St. Louis. In Section IV of his long, serious poem, "Watching Football on TV" (p. 61) he wonders if football can be compared to action in the *Iliad*. . . . "Bull-Dog!" (p. 73) was written for a 1911 song contest at Yale University by student *Cole Porter*, who had published his first song at the age of eleven. Porter went on to write fifteen thousand songs, including "Night and Day" and "I've Got You Under My Skin."

John Kieran (p. 75) covered sports for twenty-five years for the *New York Times* and the *Herald Tribune*. He gained fame on a weekly radio quiz show, "Information Please," answering tough questions about sports. . . . Young student *Scott Blaine* won a *Scholastic* magazine contest for his poem "Hockey" (p. 76).

Michael S. Harper (p. 83) has been a professor of English at Brown University since 1971. His poetry has earned him a Guggenheim Fellowship and a grant from the National Endowment for the Arts. . . . *Arnold Adoff* (p. 84) is a well-known children's poet who often writes about sports. His latest volume is *Sports Pages*. . . . "Ex-basketball Player" (p. 87) is anthologized more often than any other of *John Updike's* many poems. Three of his novels, *Rabbit Run*, *Rabbit Redux*, and *Rabbit Is Rich*, are also about an ex-basketball player. . . . *Stephen Dunn* (p. 88) played varsity basketball for Hofstra University and one year of semi-professional basketball for the Williamsport Billies in Pennsylvania. He now teaches at a college in New Jersey.

Eugene O'Neill, whose forty-five plays include *Long Day's Journey Into Night*, is viewed as America's most important playwright. He wrote his swimming poem (p. 91) as a very young newspaper reporter. . . . *Maxine Kumin* (p. 95) is an accomplished sportswoman who swims, skis, and rides horses—all in a day's work. She was written four novels, seven volumes of poetry, and seventeen books for children. Ms. Kumin also co-wrote four children's books with poet Anne Sexton (p. 102). . . . *Barbara Chesneau Lamblin* (p. 97) is an athlete writing about her sport. She swam the breast stroke on American teams in the late 1950s and early 1960s. . . . *Robert Penn Warren* (p. 104) won a Pulitzer Prize for his novel, *All the King's Men*, another for his book of poetry, *Promise*, and another for *Now and Then: Poems 1976–1978*. He taught literature for many years at Yale University and was America's first poet laureate, a title authorized by the U.S. Congress in 1976.

Shel Silverstein's *Where the Sidewalk Ends* is American's best-selling book of children's poems. Mr. Silverstein (p. 107) is also a cartoonist, playwright, and composer.

"Hazard's Optimism" by *William Meredith* (p. 112) comes from a series of sixteen poems about Hazard, a man who is painting a falling parachutist. If these poems are read one after another they have the effect of a novel.

John Gould Fletcher (p. 113) belonged to the Imagist Movement. The Imagists broke away from the tradition of telling stories and giving lectures in poetry. They advocated the use of precise images. . . . *David Daiches* (p. 115) is a Scot, not an American. But he has taught at Princeton, and the *The New Yorker* was the first to publish his "To Kate." No sports collection should go to press without it. . . . In "Skaters" (p. 117) *Vern Rutsala* writes "the rink is like a Brueghel." *William Meredith* also mentions Brueghel in "Hazard's Optimism" (p. 112). The painter Pieter Brueghel was a giant in the development of landscape painting. The small figures on his canvases are often busy playing games, hunting, skating, and dancing.

"The Sidewalk Racer" (p. 120) is a visual or "shape" poem: the way the words are placed on the pages helps express the poem's meaning. Here the words form a skateboard.

The U.S. Army's Tenth Mountain Division (p. 122) was formed during World War II. The division's newspaper, *Blizzard*, published a regular pinup picture of the Mountain of the Week. *W. T. Levitt*'s poem honors his brother, who was killed in action.

Poet *Archibald MacLeish* (p. 125) lived a public life as lawyer, professor at Harvard, Librarian of Congress, Assistant Secretary of State, and a member of the Executive Board of UNESCO. He wrote seventeen plays, among them *J.B.*, produced in New York and London. . . . *Arthur Guiterman*'s eight rowers (p. 127) are on the Hudson River.

Robinson Jeffers' poems are almost all dark and pessimistic. Compare the mood of his "Salmon-Fishing" (p. 135) to the sunnier view of fishing in *Theodore Roethke*'s "The Pike" (p. 136). . . . *Denise Pendleton*'s poem "Ice-Fishing" (p. 138) won the Washington University prize for best student poem of 1982.

Father *Thomas Merton* (p. 143) lived for twenty-seven years as a Trappist monk in Our Lady of Gethsemani, Kentucky. There he wrote prose and poetry and translated poetry from various languages into English.

Cassius Clay, described in the poem by R. Ernest Holmes (p. 144), became a Black Muslim in the middle of his boxing career and changed his name to Muhammad Ali (p. 146). . . . Poet *Charles Bukowski* (p. 148) prides himself on the tough-guy image found in all of his forty books of poetry. He has spent most of his life in California. . . . *Jack Dempsey* and *Luis Firpo* (p. 150) fought for the world heavyweight championship in September, 1923. Dempsey knocked Firpo out with a right and left to the jaw in the second round.

An Olympic event from 1904 through 1920, the tug of war (p. 157) is now an event of sorority and fraternity outings and of neighborhood picnics.

Poet *Richard Armour* (p. 158) wrote thousands of humorous poems. Some of his sports poems were published in *Sports Illustrated* and later collected in his volume *All in Sport*.

E. B. White (p. 160) is best known among young people for his classic novel *Charlotte's Web*. Older readers followed for years his essays in the *New Yorker*. He received a Pulitzer Prize in 1978 for the full body of his work.

In the early 1900s newspapers published the preachy, sentimental—and wildly popular—poems of *Edgar A. Guest* (p. 164). His first book of poems, *A Heap O' Livin'*, became a runaway best seller.

Anyone can *find* a poem! *Ted Kooser* (p. 167) noticed a rhythm, a rhyme, a double meaning (the word "strike"), and other poetical elements on a message pinned to a bulletin board.

Marge Piercy (p. 173) writes poetry and novels that champion women's liberation. Her latest book, an anthology, is *Early Ripening*, a collection of American women's poetry. . . . "Strategy for a Marathon" (p. 180) is a short section from a 372-line poem about the New York Marathon, which the poet *Marnie Mueller* ran in 1977 and 1978. Her best time for the twenty-six-mile race was four hours and fifteen minutes. . . . *Grace Butcher* (p. 185) has been competing in foot races for forty years. Recently she began racing motorcycles (p. 189). She teaches English and coaches the men's and women's cross-country running team at the Geauga Campus of Kent State University. . . . *Donald Finkle* (p. 183) has also written about hunting, bull fighting, and trampolining. A good sampling of his poetry can be found in his *Selected Shorter Poems*. . . . *Richard Wilbur* (p. 184) is the current poet laureate of America.

The standing broad jump (p. 187) was an Olympic event from 1900 through 1912. An American holds the Olympic record: 11 feet, 4⅞ inches.

James Whitcomb Riley's homespun rhymes (p. 191) and his storylines about country children made him a beloved poet of nineteenth-century America. He created the character "Little Orphant Annie" and wrote the often-memorized poem "When the Frost Is on the Punkin." Yale University gave him an honorary degree in letters. The National Institute of Arts and Letters awarded him a gold medal.

John Berryman's deadly serious poem (p. 199) uses a ball as a symbol for loss of every kind. The "he" and "I" in the poem seem to be the same person—the poet. Berryman is known as a "confessional" poet.

———————

May Swenson, a Chancellor of the Academy of American Poets, has written ten volumes of poems for children and adults, including *New and Selected Things Taking Place*, published in 1978, and her latest book, *In Other Words*, published in 1987. Most recent among her numerous and distinguished awards is a 1987 MacArthur Foundation Grant.

R. R. Knudson has been an afficionado of sports, literature, and sports literature since her youth. She is the author of the popular Zan series of sports novels for children as well as many other stories, novels, and works of non-fiction on and about athletes and the sports they play.

Acknowledgments

The editors and Orchard Press herewith render thanks to the following poets, publishers, and agents whose interest, cooperation, and permission to reprint have made possible the preparation of *American Sports Poems*. All possible care has been taken to trace the ownership of every selection included and to make a full acknowledgment for its use. If any errors have accidently occurred they will be corrected in subsequent editions, provided notification is sent to the publisher. Permission to reprint copyrighted poems is gratefully acknowledged from the following:

American Play Company, Inc. for "Babe Ruth" from *Poems for Men* by Damon Runyon (Hawthorne Books, Inc. of A. S. Barns).

Atheneum Publishers (an imprint of Macmillan, Inc.) for "Surf-Casting" from *Writing to an Unfinished Accompaniment*, copyright © 1973 by W.S. Merwin; "Interview with a Winner" from *A Mote in Heaven's Eye* (1975) in the compilation *Selected Short Poems*, copyright © 1986 by Donald Finkel; and "High Dive" from *Selected Poems* by Robert Watson, copyright © 1974 by Robert Watson.

Kevin Bezner for "The Kid."

BkMk Press, University of Missouri, Kansas City, and Samella Myers Gates for "You've Got to Learn the White Man's Game" from *Selected Poems of Mbembe Milton Smith*.

Black Sparrow Press for "The Loser" by Charles Bukowski, copyright © 1962.

Laurel Blossom for "Skate" from *What's Wrong* (The Rowfant Club Cleveland, 1987).

Brandt and Brandt Literary Agents, Inc. for "Twin Lakes Hunter" by A.B. Guthrie.

Grace Butcher for "Young Wrestlers" from *Rumors of Ecstasy . . . Rumors of Death* (Barnwood Press, 1981), first published in *Hiram Poetry Review*; for "Motorcycle Racer Thinks of Quitting"; and "Hurdler."

Henry Carlile for "Fish Story."

Chappell/Intersong for "Bull-Dog!" by Cole Porter, copyright © 1911 by Chappell and Co., Inc., copyright renewed, international copyright secured, all rights reserved.

Tom Clark for "The Last Baseball Samurai."

Billy Collins for "High Stick."

Curtis Brown, Ltd. for "Jackie Robinson" from *An Ordinary Woman* by Lucille Clifton, copyright © 1974 by Lucille Clifton; "Billy Ray Smith" by Ogden Nash, copyright ©

Author and Title Index

Subject Index